Selling the 90s:

A Decade of Riding the Wave
from Tie-Dyes to Comic Books
to Beanie Babies to Pokémon
and Everything in Between.

D0169949

Written by
Eric S. Siegel
and
James A. Siegel

HUDSON VALLEY ORGANIC PRESS

We dedicate this book to Stan Lee. His stories have entertained and inspired both of us throughout our lives. May the characters he created live on forever.

- Eric and James

Introduction

My name is James Siegel. I was born in 1991. Yesterday I played a few games of *Magic: The Gathering* at my friend's house, came home, threw on the *Pokémon* cartoon while I played the handheld video game, then read a few comic books before going to bed. I wrote that today, in the 21st century, at 26 years of age, though it could have easily been 20 years ago. My tastes haven't changed much since the 90s, except now I watch *Pokémon* on Netflix instead of waiting until Saturday morning. When *Pokémon* came out, there were 150 Pokémon. For us, it was a finite number and any kid worth their salt could name, and catch, them all. Now, after the release of hundreds more Pokémon over the years, we realize that there are an infinite number of Pokémon. We just haven't met them all yet.

When *Pokémon* first came out, I wasn't interested. That was what all the kids were into, and I thought I was too cool for that. It was my dad who made me sit down and watch an episode of the cartoon. He said all the kids liked it and I would too. I begrudgingly sat and watched as a Pokémon named Jigglypuff lost its voice. It brought me to tears, and I have loved *Pokémon* ever since. I *needed* Jigglypuff in my life after that.

Fortunately, I didn't even have to leave my home to find all the latest *Pokémon* merchandise. My dad had a store in Hackettstown, New Jersey, called Collectibles: Cards, Games, and Comics, and we had a small apartment connected to the store. So if I say I lived at that store, I mean it literally!

At that time, there weren't a lot of *Pokémon* products in the United States, but my dad carried whatever was available, much of it coming straight from Japan. That seems crazy now, given how popular *Pokémon* has become in the U.S. and worldwide, but back then the only Jigglypuff item was a set of stickers with Japanese writing on the package. My dad had the stickers in his store, and I claimed a set for myself. And thus, my *Pokémon* obsession began.

As a kid, I never realized how good I had it. Lots of kids my age grew up with Pokémon, Power Rangers, comic books, and sports cards. But few were surrounded by them like I was. All the cool new stuff that kids wanted would already be on the shelves in Collectibles: Cards Games and Comics by the time I knew I wanted it.

I didn't have to ask Santa to get me a Furby for Christmas. I went shopping at Toy R' Us with my dad until our truck was full of Furbys, to be resold at our store. My enthusiasm for my own Furby was very short lived. The damn thing kept waking me up in the the middle of the night to tell me that it loved me. I wound up throwing it against the wall in a frenzy, until the life left its creepy little eyes. My fun with the Furby lasted only a few days, but it didn't matter. By then I was already onto the next hot thing, loved and forgotten just as quickly.

All these phenomena seemed evanescent to me, and to the world at large. With a hundred brands dying for every one that made it to the next year, many were. I, like most kids, always wanted 'It', whatever cool, new thing everyone had to have at that moment.

But nowadays we can have them all, the tradeoff being that none of them are 'It' anymore. New *Magic:The Gathering* sets keep making my decks stronger and stronger. I recently bought a Gameboy Advance again, loaded up *Pokémon: Leaf Green*, and set off to catch all 150 original Pokémon again. Many of the comic books I loved as a kid have been rebooted, sometimes within the books, but more often these now-timeless tales have been adapted on TV or in movies.

For better or worse, the so called "geek" and "nerd" culture has left the comic shop far behind. Oh, you'll still find us geeks and nerds rolling d20s in the back of comic and game stores nationwide, but you'll also find us everywhere else, proudly sporting licensed T-shirts of our favorite retro characters. While I was growing up, teens or adults would be scoffed at for publicly announcing that they collect comics or play a trading card game, but now all those things have become accepted, part of the mainstream of our cultural heritage.

Last week I bought a full-priced Beanie Baby for the first time in over a decade. It was Spider-Man, the first time I ever saw an officially licensed superhero Beanie. I had to buy it. Everything looks different, but nothing has changed.

Like many children of the 90s, I never truly left the era behind. In the early 2000s, when I was in middle school I found a sealed box of Power Rangers pogs tucked away in a closet and started a pog revival at school overnight. As soon as kids saw me playing pogs with my friends, everybody started digging out their old pogs and we had some great games. In pogs, you play for keeps and can get a cool mix of all your friends' pogs. Unfortunately, this can lead to bad feelings, and our pog revival was shot down shortly after it started when some kid complained to the principal that he had lost all his pogs on the playground. But I will always remember those games of pogs, even fonder than my memories of pogs during their breakout popularity in the 90s.

In this book, nostalgia is not just an elephant in the room. Nostalgia is sometimes considered a dirty word, as it is often used to shill shallow Star Wars spinoffs and the like. But this book *is* nostalgia, a trip down memory lane for all of us who were kids, teens, or collectible-craving adults in the 1990s.

This book is my dad's story. Aside from this introduction, it is told from his perspective, but it is the story of my childhood as well. We worked on every part of this book together, reminding each other of countless memories. Good memories, bad memories, and some that were downright ugly.

But that is why we embrace nostalgia head-on, and when it comes to comics, games, toys, all that stuff I loved as a kid, my perspective on them all is just as knowingly nostalgic. The nice thing is that now the modern fan can choose to put on the rose-tinted glasses and look back on those days so easily. We can romanticize that manic search from store to store, seeking that one issue or card we needed, because now we can buy it with one click on eBay, often for less than we paid back then!

A product of my generation, I appreciate modern conveniences more than anything. I realize it most when I'm playing my favorite SEGA Genesis games. I'll get to a place where I would get stuck as a kid, never able to figure out how to proceed further. Back then, it was just me and the game -- if I couldn't figure it out, the game was over. Now, smart phone in hand, I can simply search out a video on YouTube that will show me exactly what I need to do to move on. Phones didn't do that back then.

This book begins before I was born, and, as I was writing it, I remembered more and more as the years wore on. Some watched these phenomena come and go. I mostly just watched them go.

I cannot recall a time before *Magic: The Gathering*, and it has always been my favorite game. Even before I could read, I "played" *Magic*, or at least played with the cards. I remember my first deck, which was just a stack of cards that had art I liked. I looked up to the *Magic* players, able to match wits and cast powerful spells and creatures like the highly coveted Shivan Dragon. I was determined to learn how to play, and gain the ability to drop fearsome dragons of my own.

Now, over two decades later, I have a bunch of Shivan Dragons. The first dragon ever printed in *Magic*, the Shivan Dragon appeared in the very first set, and used to fetch a hefty sum. They are worth less than a dollar now, having been reprinted many times over the years, and it is not a very powerful or useful card in the modern game, compared to the fearsome new dragons they dream up now. But even if they were worthless, I'd still jam one in my deck, because the Shivan Dragon will always be cool to me.

And that's kind of the point, isn't it? Casting the Shivan Dragon today takes me back, gives me a taste of the power that seemed to crackle all around me as a kid. The simple joys of youth can be recreated today with a Google search and a credit card. We choose to put on those rose-tinted glasses -- or to us *Magic* players, the Sunglasses of Urza.

I often like to view the 90s in that way. Reading a comic book, action figure in hand, Nirvana or Smashing Pumpkins on the radio, soaking it all in. That was the reality, but there was more to it. Comic books may have taught me how to read, but the issues I grew up with are long gone. Everything got sold.

On one hand, I had it better than anyone, even hardcore collectors, because I had access to *everything.* Every single week, stacks of new comics arrived, more than could ever be read in a mere seven days. But they would be gone the next week, replaced with a new stack. Most people who visited our stores would go home with a bagful of physical memories, stuff that would continue to remind them of the time of their life when they bought it. I had it all, but all I took away were the memories. Of course, if everyone else had held onto everything they bought back then, there would be very little interest in it today.

Maybe you remember when every kid *had* to have a Charizard. I was one of those kids. I got a box of the original *Pokémon* trading cards for my birthday, and pulling a Charizard out of one of the packs was an unforgettable moment. It was emblematic of the sheer and simple joy of cracking open a pack, that moment you get just want you wanted. That triumphant feeling was invariably worth far more than the price of the pack itself. So it felt amazing to pull a Charizard on my birthday. But I didn't keep it for long.

Charizard isn't exactly the best *Pokémon* card. It was the most sought after, and it fetched the highest prices, but in terms of gameplay value, Charizard was never the best. So, as soon as the joy of cracking my first Charizard wore off, I got rid of it. I traded it to another kid for about 50 other rare cards. Monetarily, it was a fair deal at the time, but we each walked away feeling like we had ripped off the other. While that Charizard is now worth much more than the value of the stack of random stuff I traded it for, I have always stood by that deal. Instead of one powerful card, I gained dozens of powerful new cards and upgraded *all* my decks.

I was of the perfect age to be a player of *Pokémon* first, not a collector. Some kids had a lot of money tied up in binders full of expensive cards they never used because they didn't know how to play the game. While there is nothing wrong with just collecting, I was always totally hands-on, not just with *Pokémon* but with everything. Despite knowing better, I always ripped the tags off my Beanie Babies, immediately devaluing them, but making them all the more lovable. I never kept a toy in the package. Everything I owned was used, played with, loved, and abused. And, in the end, it was all sold.

My Magic decks are stronger than ever. I have gotten further in *Pokémon* video games in recent years than I ever could as a kid. I still love Jigglypuff, and I have a very huggable stuffed Jigglypuff in my room. My comic book collection is impressive, overflowing with gems new and old. I still try to read a couple issues every day. My floor isn't covered with action figures like it was for most of my youth, but a few notable figures can be spotted around my room. Heck, even that new Spider-Man Beanie Baby I bought still has the tag on it! I pretty much still love the same things I did twenty years ago – but nothing I have now is what I owned twenty years ago.

The cards, comics, toys, and everything of my youth has been sold. Even the faded and tagless Beanie Babies that filled my bed for years were flipped at a flea market somewhere along the way. And I never minded a bit. What *Star Trek*'s entrepreneurial Ferengi called the Great Material Continuum, the river of items to be bought and sold, kept my family's life in motion. The reason I was able to read so many comic books is *because* they all got sold, supplying my family's livelihood and keeping the stream of merchandise flowing. That was just the way things were. Although I approached something like *Pokémon* as a game first, I always understood it as a product as well.

I never saw the treasures of my youth as priceless. In fact, I could almost always tell you what the price was.

Chapter 1

My name is Eric Siegel. I was born in 1962. My grandfather owned a luncheonette in the Bronx while I was growing up. He made burgers, fries, and milkshakes, and also sold candy, cigarettes, magazines, and most importantly, comic books. I was basically raised in that store up until the age of eight. Both of my parents worked full time, so I spent most of my days there. When I reached school age, I took the subway to the luncheonette after getting out of school each day.

Since before I can even remember, I was drawn to the comic books in my grandfather's luncheonette. They sold for 12 cents in those days. During the countless hours I spent at the store, I read the comics on the shelf over and over, every day without fail.

At first, I loved war comic books the most. This probably has something to do with the Vietnam War going on at that time, slipping its way into my unconsciousness. Whatever the cause, I have always had a morbid fascination with war, starting with those comics. *Sgt. Rock* was my favorite, followed by *Sgt. Fury and his Howling Commandos*. I also loved *The Unknown Soldier* and *The Haunted Tank*. There were plenty of superhero comics as well, but I didn't like those as much. They weren't the ones I wanted to reread again and again. Even though the war comic stories were all basically the same, for years there was nothing more exciting to me than a new issue of one of those titles.

While I didn't read superhero comics often, I loved some of the covers because of the colorful art. As a second grader, I once traded a copy of *Fantastic Four* for two war comics. Even though I liked the comics I got, I always regretted making that trade because I liked the cover of that issue so much.

My disappointment after parting with that issue felt strange, so the next time I got a *Fantastic Four* comic, I made sure to actually read it. Not only did that one have another cool cover, but the story was awesome! It was a cosmic adventure, which seemed much more interesting than the repetitive war stories I was used to. The superheroes grew on me after that. The Fantastic Four were my favorites but I also really liked Iron Man and the Hulk at a very young age.

For the first few years of school, I would work in my grandfather's store in the afternoons and was rewarded with stacks of comics. He gave me the ones that didn't sell and he received a credit from the distributor for them. Normally those unsold comics were just thrown away so it worked out well for both of us.

I was able to accumulate quite a few comics this way, which laid the foundation for my collection. Sadly, my grandfather shut down his store during the summer before I started fifth grade. He had been robbed too many times, even shot once or twice. Although my love of comics was born in my grandfather's luncheonette, it surely did not die when the store did.

Shortly after my grandfather closed up shop, my parents decided to move. After a brief time in Mt. Vernon, a suburb of New York City, we settled down in Dobbs Ferry, another nearby suburb. My parents gave me five dollars each day to feed myself and my younger brother Owen. Owen and I would spend two or three dollars on pizza or fast food, and keep the rest for comics.

Over several years we were able to build up large collections. The cover price for the average superhero comic at the time was 20 cents, but for a quarter you could get a DC giant-sized issue. Even though they cost a bit more, I always made sure to buy the Batman and Justice League giant-sized issues because they were packed full of fun and excitement.

In addition to the comics we bought with our surplus food money, my father would sometimes bring stuff for us back from Manhattan, where he worked. He was able to get some of the older 12-cent back issues for 50 cents each. *Fantastic Four*, *X-Men*, and *Justice League of America* were now my favorites, while my brother preferred *The Amazing Spider-Man*. By 1975, with our father's help in getting some of the earlier issues, we had acquired nearly complete runs of all those titles.

A year later Dad took us to ComicCon in the Penta Hotel on 34th street. This was a defining moment in my love for comic books. I got to meet

Stan Lee, the famous creator of all our favorite characters! He was riding the elevator with Jim Shooter, another legendary comic book creator. This certainly cemented my love of comics, only increasing the fervor with which I sought them out.

By the time I was thirteen I was working part-time after school. I was a dishwasher throughout high school, providing a steady cash flow to keep buying comics. My X-Men and Fantastic Four collections grew steadily. It got to the point that when the cover price was 50 cents, around 1979 to 1980, I was so into the X-Men that I was buying five to ten copies of each issue as they came out. My brother did the same with Spider-Man for a while, but he eventually lost interest. That led to me buying out his collection, as I had done with all of my friends' collections as well. Needless to say, I had a ton of comics.

After high school, I managed to keep buying and collecting comics no matter where I was. I joined the Navy and served on an aircraft carrier, which made getting my comic books challenging. Although it was impossible to get new issues while I was out at sea, I did whatever I could to make sure I kept up with my favorite titles. When the ship docked in our home port outside of Jacksonville, Florida, I took two long bus rides to get to a comic store in downtown Jacksonville.

My favorite characters during my Navy years were Spider-Man, the X-Men, Conan the Barbarian, and Batman. The owner of the shop kept a box put aside for me where he'd add a copy of each new release. Even when I was out at sea for months, I didn't miss an issue.

Living on a ship, there was not much room to store my comics and there was always the risk they'd get stolen. Whenever I amassed about fifty books, I'd ship them back home to my parents where they would be safe. I always made sure to bag and board my comics, taping the back shut to keep them in good condition.

One of the main reasons that old comics are so valuable is that people didn't take very good care of them. They let them get tarnished or thrown away. During my childhood there were very few supplies to protect comic books, which is why finding those issues in good condition is so hard. I always made sure to keep my comics in the best condition possible, whether on land or at sea.

After the Navy, I went to the State University of New York at New Paltz for a few years. I took a student job there so I had some spending money. There was a great comic book store in town, just a five-minute walk from the campus.

That is when I started to ramp up my buying, picking up ten copies of every X-Men and Spider-Man title published between 1984 and 1986. I'd also buy plenty of other new releases every week, just not in multiples. This was shortly before the comic book boom, while the general public was still not paying much attention to superheroes.

Eventually there came a point when comic books were truly the center of my life, in a way I never could have imagined. But before I made my livelihood selling comic books, I sold tie-dyes.

Chapter 2

When I was twenty-five I decided to take a
semester off from college. After I got out of the
Navy, getting a degree seemed like the next logical
step, but I decided that college was not for me. I
didn't like studying and taking tests one bit. What I
did love was going out and partying.

I stopped taking classes, but I wanted to stay
in New Paltz so I found work as a roofer's assistant.
I didn't like roofing and wasn't much good at it, but
it paid $75 cash plus lunch every day. In my first few
months I managed to staple my finger, fall through a
skylight, and almost kill my boss by knocking a box
of nails off a roof. Roofing, like college, was also not
for me.

My apartment building was next to a tie-dye
shop called Not Fade Away. They were a new
business, having been open less than a year. One
morning I saw a "Help Wanted" sign in the store
window and went in to ask about it. Luckily for me,
the manager was a former roofer from Missouri who
sympathized with my situation. He hired me on the
spot, saying, "If you can do roofing, you can make
tie-dyes."

And I could. It was a minimum wage job,
paying just half of what I had earned as a roofer. I
didn't mind. I got to work with lots of pretty girls,
and it was far better than being on a hot roof all day.
I became quite good at making tie-dyes. At the
time, Not Fade Away consisted of that small retail

store with a three-story factory. The main place these shirts were sold was at Grateful Dead concerts.

The Grateful Dead had been releasing music and touring regularly since I was a small child, but they had a huge resurgence in the 1980s, due in large part to their 1987 hit, "Touch of Gray". With a music video in heavy rotation on MTV, the song was the Dead's first top ten hit since 1970. It created thousands of new Grateful Dead fans, who came out in droves to see the band play live.

The most devout of these fans, the so-called "Deadheads", followed the band on their concert tours around the country so they could see every show. This unique lifestyle created some equally unique business opportunities. And without a doubt the most important of these ventures was making and selling the Deadhead uniform of choice: tie-dyes. These brightly colored, kaleidoscopic shirts are the visual equivalent of the Dead's psychedelic music.

When I started at Not Fade Away, tie-dyes were on the brink of becoming a craze. Half of the staff was out on tour selling shirts, and they needed help making more. The company had also recently signed a huge contract with Macy's for thousands of tie-dyed slouch socks. Between the socks and the shirts, which kept selling out on tour, demand for the product was enormous. We were the largest manufacturer of tie-dyes at the time, and all of our products were handcrafted.

These were not the old school tie-dyes of my childhood. These were made from white, 100% cotton clothing, using high concentrations of professional grade dye, tied with sailor's twine. In addition, Not Fade Away had a license to use official Grateful Dead logos and imagery.

The average licensed shirt sold for $35 in 1987. Those were our most popular products, but we also sold regular tie-dyes for $10 to $20, depending on the difficulty of the design. For $10 you would get something simple, like a rainbow spiral. For $15 you could get a peace sign or a smiley face tied into the shirt. The $20 shirts had more elaborate designs like shooting star patterns.

The first time I went to a show to sell tie-dyes, we didn't have any of the licensed shirts. I was sent to the Meadowlands in New Jersey with another Not Fade Away employee, Dan. We were given two duffel bags filled with the $10, $15, and $20 tie dyes and told we could keep 10 percent of the sales. We arrived, paid $6 for parking, and checked out the scene.

This was the same stadium where the New York Giants football team played, and it was like a tailgating party on hallucinogenics. The parking lot seemed like one big festival, but as we walked around we also noticed people getting busted by undercover cops for trying to sell stuff. We decided not to try setting up.

After wandering around for a while, we were pretty much ready to give up. That's when we stumbled upon parking lot 18, where vending was allowed. We dragged the heavy duffel bags out there and found a good spot, laid down a tarp, and set up the shirts. There were still a couple hours before the Grateful Dead were slated to play.

The shirts started selling as soon as we set up shop. An hour into the concert we were completely sold out. We continued to hang out in the parking lot, listening to the music and enjoying the party. After selling $2400 worth of tie-dyes, we each made $120 in cash. I knew I was onto something good.

After the success of that night I began spending less time making shirts and more time selling them. I soon found that I was not the only one making a living on the road. There must have been hundreds of vendors in the loose caravan that followed the Dead from city to city. Everyone would set up in the parking lot, making a little shopping area outside the concert. That area was, and in some circles still is, known as Shakedown Street, after the Grateful Dead song and album.

For the most part, the local police and stadium security just let it happen. Undercover cops went through the crowd busting anyone they caught selling drugs, but the average merchandise seller was left alone. Most of the vendors were just Deadheads selling food, trying to survive and make it to the next show.

Accordingly, most of the food I ate came from Shakedown Street. I tried to support the real Deadheads who had been on tour for years. There were whole families -- small children included -- that followed the Dead in vans or school buses, selling food at each stop. You could get a grilled cheese sandwich for $1, a kind veggie burrito for $2, or a big bowl of rasta pasta for $3. People also happily traded food for tie-dyes. Some also sold cold beer, but those people would often get busted.

It was a very strange economy out there on tour. One familiar face, a tattered-looking hippie with long hair and a longer beard, would amble through the crowd asking, "Got a dollar?" I stopped him at a show one day and gave him a few bucks to hear his story. He told me that he hailed from the Florida panhandle and owned a brand new Corvette. While on tour he made his living merely by asking for a dollar. He didn't beg. With the huge crowds at the Dead shows, he did very well for himself, just walking around saying, "Got a dollar?"

Most of my coworkers closed down when the concert started. As for me, while I have been to over 100 shows, I have only gone inside to see the band play eight times. This is because there was still a lot of money left to be made once the show started, especially from locals who were not able to get in. They spent the money they had planned to use for a ticket, content with buying a souvenir as consolation. The scene in the parking lot was usually a lot of fun and you could almost always hear the music anyway, so I didn't see much reason to go in. The only times I went inside were those nights when the weather was unbearable.

One such instance occurred in Hartford, Connecticut. We brought fifteen duffel bags full of shirts to sell. We arrived at noon and sales were great early on, despite temperatures in the twenties. Around 7 PM, freezing rain arrived and cleared everyone out. The person I was manning the booth with insisted we go inside so we broke it down.

Not Fade Away always had tickets put aside for employees, and while we did have to pay for them, the seats were very good. At one point Jerry Garcia started losing his voice. Martin, one of the owners of Not Fade Away, passed a bottle of honey loquat syrup up to him. This seemed to do the trick and the rest of the show went on flawlessly.

Working for Not Fade away was a great opportunity, and I did not take it for granted. Since I was a good and honest salesman, they sent me to dozens of shows. It was much more fun than anything that I had previously done, and I made good money. However, the 1988 Grateful Dead tour was the last one I did working for Not Fade Away.

Martin and Dean, Not Fade Away's owners, had brought high quality tie-dying to New Paltz and the Dead tour. They had learned their advanced techniques from living in a hippy community in Tennessee called "The Farm". It was there that tie-dying truly evolved. Just as Martin and Dean started Not Fade Away using what they had learned from the old hippies, I decided to take everything I had learned about making and selling tie-dyes, and go into business for myself.

Chapter 3

I decided to go it alone on the 1989 Dead tour. I had already learned every aspect of the business and knew I was good at it. I started making tie-dyes right in my studio apartment. After I tied and dyed them, the shirts needed 24 hours for the dye to set before being rinsed. I had acquired a Crescor, a rack used in the food service industry to hold trays. Instead of food, I stored my freshly-dyed shirts on baking sheets in my Crescor, then brought them to the basement laundry room late at night for the rinse. My manufacturing operation certainly wasn't as professional as Not Fade Away -- but my shirts were also top-notch.

I named my company "Color Explosion", and spent all the money I had on high-quality supplies. Then I hit the road. Selling tie-dyes on the Dead tour could be profitable and fun but it wasn't easy. You never knew what the weather was going to be like. Sometimes, if the rain was bad enough, you could lose an entire day. It can also get really cold out there. You might make a few sales in zero-degree weather, but is it worth freezing for hours to sell two or three shirts? That was always the dilemma.

Then there was the danger of getting busted. During the '89 tour, some Washington, DC motorcycle cops shook me down. They were hassling all the vendors for whatever they could get, goods or money. Some fools gave them cash, but I only offered some tie-dyed panties for their girlfriends and got clear without much of a loss. A few weeks later, in Atlanta, I caught someone trying to steal my truck. There were always risks on the road.

Other vendors from New Paltz also went on tour, and they didn't always have the best of luck either. A vendor named Ron, who sold Guatemalan clothing, left his money belt at a diner in South Carolina. It held every cent he had to his name. When he discovered his loss, he drove four hours back to that diner, to no avail.

A guy named Mario had his van blow its engine at a Stuckey's restaurant in Oine, North Carolina. He was fortunate enough to run into some Deadheads there a little later and was able to continue on tour. But he never got his van back, it was stuck at Stuckey's.

I heard countless stories of vendors getting robbed. I always made sure to regularly stop by a bank and turn my cash into traveler's checks, which I sent to my post office box back home. Luckily, I never did get robbed, but I was always careful not to have too much cash on me just to be safe.

To make it worth the trip, you had to be inventive with how you made money. If the concert was at a venue that didn't allow vending, I would sometimes stuff a backpack full of shirts and try to sell them as inconspicuously as possible. This led to several close calls where I had to run -- but it was better to take the risk and make a few bucks than make nothing at all.

It was also hard to judge how much product you'd need and space was limited, and sometimes you'd sell out. Once when the Dead were playing three days in a row in Atlanta, I sold out of tie-dyes the first day. I was 900 miles from home and there were still two days of huge crowds ahead. The next morning I went to Sam's Club and bought M&M's in bulk. They cost me 25 cents a pack and I sold them for $1. I would simply walk around the crowd saying, "M&M's, plain or peanut." In two days I sold close to 500 packs. From then on, I would do this whenever I ran out of merchandise.

Making a profit selling tie-dyes on the Dead tour required a grueling schedule, and it began to take a toll on me. As a one-man operation, I would have to start making more shirts as soon as I got home. Once I had a big enough batch of tie-dyes, it was back to the road again. My biggest issue was all the time wasted traveling to far away shows.

I started to look for different kinds of venues to sell my wares. Tie-dyes were becoming popular with more than just hippies. If I could find places to sell close to home, that would mean less time traveling and more time making shirts.

First, I tried craft shows at churches. They charged $10 to $15 for a spot so it was a low-risk experiment. I have never been the typical church-going type, especially back then when I had long, messy hair and wore tie-dyes from head to toe. As I did on tour, I always brought along a boom box and played Grateful Dead music. I certainly looked out of place next to a bunch of women with country crafts and glue guns, but the spectacle only helped sales.

I also tried some mall craft shows. These cost considerably more, sometimes as much as $100 for a booth, but they also had potential to be much more profitable. There were tight restrictions on what kinds of products could be sold at these shows. I was able to get around those restrictions most of the time because my products were technically handmade, though plenty of the old ladies next to me would scoff and complain about my setup.

I made some money with the craft shows and some Christmas fairs, but I found something better in the spring of 1990: flea markets.

The flea market is something of an American tradition, if not necessarily a proud one. The first one I tried was a small weekly Saturday market in Woodstock, New York, just forty minutes from New Paltz. While the famous 1969 music festival was not actually held in Woodstock, it did inspire the name. With that cultural heritage, it came as no surprise that tie-dyes sold very well there.

There were stores in Woodstock that sold tie-dyes, but mine were of equal quality or better -- and much cheaper! Tourists came to Woodstock from everywhere, many of them with the specific intention of buying tie-dyes. I had a huge setup. I rented two spots for $20 each and could make up to

$800 in sales. I wasn't able to break for lunch. I got a local kid to bring me food from Taco Juan's, the Mexican restaurant in town. This was the peak of the tie-dye craze, and it was always a good day out there.

The Woodstock flea market was small and pleasant, just thirty to forty vendors in a grassy field. It was a far cry from some of the huge parking lot flea markets that soon became my main source of income.

There was another guy making and selling tie-dyes in Woodstock, who I got to know to know far better than I wanted to. Timothy did excellent work, and was capable of making some designs that were beyond my ability, such as double shooting stars and Jerry Garcia's face. When I needed extra product, I bought from him. His top tier designs fetched up to $40 each because they were so time consuming and difficult to produce. He sold on the Dead tour as well, and continued to do it long after I stopped.

Once when I was between apartments, I stayed at Timothy's house for a month. It was good because he let me do my tie-dying there. On the other hand, it was also extremely bizarre. One of the first things he did when I moved in was warn me not to drink from the bottle of Bacardi in the fridge because it was LSD. He had a degree in chemistry and made the acid himself.

Timothy tripped frequently during my month there. His room was filled with small tables covered with all kinds of crystals -- tourmaline, amethyst, you name it. Some were massive, up to four feet high. He loved to drop acid and just sit around listening to the Dead, staring at his crystals.

While some parts of Timothy's hippie lifestyle were cool, others were much less so. For instance, there were nasty enema bottles hanging in his shower. He used to take a coffee enema every morning -- using organic coffee, of course. I never showered once during that month. He also constantly walked around naked. His girlfriend came over on the weekends and joined him in nudity. She was not a hippie, she had some kind of corporate job in Manhattan. There was a lot of weirdness going on.

Whatever crazy situation I found myself in, I still managed to keep the cash flowing. I was always looking for new things to sell, and new places to sell them. One way I expanded was by adding more products. Soon I was tie-dying everything, and kids and baby items rapidly became the most popular items. I was just about the only one making these at the time, and the kids really did look cute in them. It worked great for me because I could make larger batches of smaller clothes. Soon I was pumping out all kinds of clothing, and the regular shirts were just part of my setup. Anything white and 100% cotton could be tie-dyed, and usually was.

For a while I also vended at football games. For these I made special, team-specific products. Almost every Sunday of the season, there was a pro football game at the Meadowlands, less than two hours away. For the football fans, gloves were the best-selling product. I made red and blue pairs for the Giants, and green and white ones for the Jets. These were just thin cotton gloves that I dyed in large batches.

I got to the stadium early and walked around the parking lots, where people were tailgating. People out there were usually drunk and cold. Those gloves sold really well. They only cost about $2 a pair to make and I sold them for $5 a pair. I always liked to wear a pair myself, though I had to cut the finger parts off so I could make change. But overall, it was great advertising that also kept me somewhat warm.

My best day with the gloves was a playoff game between the Giants and the Bears in December of 1990. It was about ten degrees and very windy. I sold over 300 pairs of gloves. However, I did get busted that day.

I only kept about twenty pairs on me at a time, leaving the rest in my truck. So although I lost one bag of gloves to the Meadowlands security guards, I didn't lose all of them. They kept me detained for about an hour. Then they took my picture, said if I got caught again they would press charges with the State Police, and then they let me go. I had bought a ticket before my brief incarceration, so I was still able to see the game.

On Fridays when I had no other market to go to, I took a train down to New York City with a garbage bag full of shirts. I'd find somewhere to set up on St. Mark's Place in Greenwich Village. Then I'd cut up the garbage bag to make a large surface area to display my products. There were always vendors selling on the street around there, and keeping a few to either side of me helped me avoid police for the most part. I could get $200 to $400 in sales in a night out there. Fridays in the city were especially helpful when there was rain in the weekend forecast, so I could still make some cash.

Tie-dyes were certainly my main focus during this time, but I always stocked a few complementary products. A friend of mine made crystal necklaces that he sold to me for $60 per dozen. I sold them for $10 each. I also kept a display of Guatemalan bracelets that I bought for 25 cents and sold for $1.

Then there were Grateful Dead cassette tapes. I paid $100 for a rack that came preloaded with 75 high-quality concert recordings. I had a double cassette deck and would crank out copies of the tapes all day long. They sold great at $5. I was also more than happy to trade one of mine for a good recording of a show I didn't have. This also meant that I could blast the Grateful Dead's music wherever I was selling, which certainly helped attract customers.

Keeping an eye out for new and interesting products has always been a key to my success. If I only sold one type of merchandise, I might have been out of business a long time ago. Though tie-dyes were hugely successful for a few years, it was clear that the trend couldn't last forever.

When I started Color Explosion in 1989, the Grateful Dead and the associated culture, including tie-dyes, were at their peak. In 1990, I only did the East Coast leg of the Dead tour, while expanding my non-clothing merchandise section all the time. That was my last full year making and selling tie-dyes, though I'd continue selling various kinds of shirts for many years to come. By 1991 only half of my booth contained tie-dyes, while the rest was filled with superhero clothing and merchandise. The market was shifting, and I had to shift with it.

The 1989 Batman movie reinvigorated the public's interest in superheroes, and became a a major factor in sparking the comics boom. I already had a foot in the comic book world as a lifelong fan, so I was well equipped to make the transition to selling.

On the way to selling comic books, I started making tie-dyes with superhero themes. The most popular was a Batman onesie for babies. They were dyed black with a yellow oval on the front, upon which I would paint a bat symbol with permanent fabric paint. As time went on the superhero stuff took over more and more of my booth.

The comics boom was just around the corner. But while I was still primarily selling shirts, I found another big boom in progress: sports cards.

Chapter 4

As I continued to expand in the early 90s, I began splitting my time between New York and Florida. The first time I went down to Florida to vend was shortly after Christmas in 1989. I went to stay with my grandfather – the same one who used to own the luncheonette in the Bronx. He had moved down to Lauderdale Lakes and lived in a small one-bedroom apartment. Though he let me stay with him, it was certainly not easy, as he was really a mean old guy.

While I had a place to stay, I still had to support myself otherwise. I had brought eight duffle bags filled with tie-dyes down to Florida with me. The reason I went down there was because there was a huge flea market called the Swap Shop just a few miles from my grandfather's apartment. Located in Plantation, Florida, it was the second biggest flea market in the country, and it was open seven days a week. This gave me an opportunity I never had before, since most of my vending up until then only happened on weekends.

I was very enthusiastic about this new market, though it was far different than anything I had experienced yet. The Swap Shop was a circus, and that's not just a metaphor -- a literal circus formed part of the Swap Shop. Every day elephants paraded through the market, followed by a full circus show. The circus was held inside a big building that also housed food and high-end jewelry vendors. There were several ninety foot long tents outside, including a produce tent and an electronics tent. I always set up outside, where you could find just about any kind of junk imaginable. Once I saw a woman whose entire setup consisted of five tomatoes. I would have bought one, but they weren't even good-looking tomatoes.

If a day of circuses and shopping wasn't enough fun, at night the Swap Shop turned into a drive-in movie theater. There were fifteen screens and admission was $5 per carload. Some people would really try to get the most bang for their buck. One time I saw what must have been close to twenty people piled into, and on top of, a single station wagon!

Additionally, there were golf carts rolling through the market day and night, selling beer. Plenty of the vendors started drinking at six in the morning and were still going strong after the movies were over. Fortunately, the Florida beer was watered down. All cans and bottles had a special Florida stamp on them, confirming that they were 3.2% alcohol or lower. Standing in a parking lot in the hot Florida sun all day can definitely make you want to suck down a lot of beer, but I avoided the temptation -- for the most part.

Vendor locations inside the building were the most expensive, and it wasn't cheap in the tents either. There were tons of spots outside, however, and they cost far less. A location way on the outside of the parking lot rented for just $3. On Thursdays, the Swap Shop gave out free spots outside, and there were hundreds more vendors than any other day of the week.

Each Thursday I would get out there at 4:30 AM so I had a couple of extra hours to scout out the free areas. To try to make a living out there, I had to get the best spot I could each day of the week. As I figured out the market, I learned that I could pay in advance to reserve spots instead of just showing up and taking whatever I could get. I was able to nail down a good spot that was close to the building. It was much cheaper than actually being inside, but I got the same foot traffic as the vendors who were paying more.

My setup was a 20' by 20' square booth constructed of heavy steel fencing pipes. The legs were 6' 8" high, with a big tarp on top. I flew a 4' by 4' tie-dye wall-hanging like a flag from a PVC pipe that rose another five feet above the booth. This was soon replaced by a Batman flag. I rigged up the booth with bungee cords around three sides, from which I hung shirts with clothes pins. All of this together meant my setup looked more professional than most of the vendors around me, as well as more colorful.

The problem with the Swap Shop was that tie-dyes were not a very popular item there. The Swap Shop was a far cry from Shakedown Street, and the average customer was quite the opposite of a Deadhead. There were some tourists who came during the winter months and plenty of senior citizens year round, but most were locals whose shopping and entertainment needs were served primarily by the Swap Shop.

In this part of Florida, the highway served as an economic divide between classes. On one side of the street were gated communities where people had driveways with boats in them. On the other side, some of the people could barely afford clothes. These people were the Swap Shop's main customers, not the wealthy.

Despite not having the best product for the Swap Shop, I did fine at first. There was some novelty to the tie-dyes, and I was willing to sell them cheap. I could only sell them for about half as much as they went for in New York, which was my cost. I had to do it to make enough cash to eat. Since I still had to go through the intensive process of making the shirts even though I was selling them for the lowest price I ever had, I started looking for alternative ways to earn money.

I noticed a few people selling baseball cards out at the market, and I knew I had plenty from when I was a kid. As with comics, I had picked up most of my friends' cards when they lost interest in them. I had my dad send down a shoebox full of baseball cards.

When they arrived, I immediately bought a price guide from a sports card vendor at the Swap Shop. I nearly fainted when I saw the prices! The bulk of my collection was baseball cards from between 1969 and 1973. They had been sitting neatly lined up in a box for years and were still in pretty good shape. I had quite a few valuable cards, so I bought some hard plastic "toploader" sleeves to put them in. I was ready to make some money.

I started selling baseball cards for the first time the very next day. I used black electrical tape to secure the encased cards to the table. This caused a lot of interest out there at the Swap Shop. When I was asked the price of a card, I told them it was half of what was listed in the price guide. I was also willing to haggle at length if necessary.

I sold my most expensive card that day, a 1969 Mickey Mantle. At that time, in early 1991, the list price was $250. Mine had a little stain on it, though, so I let it go for $100. I didn't care about getting top dollar. It was found money to me, and $100 was a lot more than I made trying to sell tie-dyes.

The cards were a success right from the start, so I brought out some comics soon after. They weren't nearly as popular. Part of the problem was that I only had one box with me at the time, holding some of my best stuff from the 60s. These books were worth good money, and I wanted a premium price for them -- too high for the Swap Shop crowd. There was one guy, however, who would trade old sports cards to me for my old comics. Since the local demographic preferred cards, I was more than happy to make the trades we did.

I used to buy older cards from a guy named Sam as well. He inherited a large baseball card collection and was willing to sell the cards to me at very reasonable prices. However, I had to go to his house to buy them, and I did not like going there because Sam had a pet bobcat.

If I had had enough money, I could have just bought the whole collection and been done with it, but I couldn't afford that. I did go down to his house a few times and got some really good deals on cards that I could sell. The last time that I went down there, Sam's face and arms were all bandaged up. The bobcat got him pretty good.

Within a few weeks, sports cards became the main product in my setup. I started delving into hockey cards because of the Canadian tourists who frequented the Swap Shop. I was making money, and I was not alone. There were sometimes as many as fifty baseball card vendors out there. Soon there was a whole card section of the Swap Shop. But no matter how many new vendors would pop up, more customers would follow.

Most of the other people selling cards there were much more casual about the way they did business. I remember these three old men who were always out there with the same stuff every day. They had mostly battered old cards from when they were kids, plus a few more that they picked up somewhere along the way. While they had a decent selection, they didn't realize that their cards were in poor condition -- and getting worse daily. With no canopy to protect them, those cards were getting bleached by the sun every day. Just because you have something worth selling doesn't mean you know what you are doing.

Since I had good stock with a professional-looking booth, I quickly became one of the top sellers of sports cards in the Swap Shop. My booth changed to reflect this, with cards front and center and fewer shirts than ever.

I took my early profits from my own childhood cards and invested in new ones. I sought out a card distributor in Fort Lauderdale where I was able to get new product at wholesale prices. Soon I was getting cards by the case, and selling them by the box or pack.

I still made tie-dyes, but in ever-smaller quantities. It was to be my last year making them, though I did continue selling tie-dyes, including Timothy's, for years to come.

Shifting from shirts to cards wasn't the only change I made to my business once I started vending at the Swap Shop. During those first months I was in Florida, a storm was brewing -- Operation Desert Storm, that is. Wartime is no different than any other time: if something is consuming the public's interest, then there is always a way to make a profit from that interest.

Topps, a card company known mainly for their extensive line of sports cards, produced a set of Desert Storm trading cards. They sold briskly for higher than retail price. For a month or two Topps'

Desert Storm cards sold better than their sports cards.

With patriotism on the rise, I invested in a bunch of American flag and yellow ribbon pins, and bumper stickers with endearing slogans like "Sack Iraq". I acquired my stock from a guy who was walking around the Swap Shop one day, selling these items in bulk to vendors. He was selling them for 50¢ each. I gave him all the money I had on me, about $300.

I had no problem selling the pins and stickers at $1 apiece, happy to double my money. I always found it ironic that these items adorned with American flags were all made in China, but what can you do? Everyone was just trying to make a buck out there.

Chapter 5

My first couple of months down in Florida were quite successful. But by April, business slowed. There were fewer tourists, and the part-time residents who only lived in southern Florida during the winter started disappearing. I also decided to head north, back to New York.

I returned and started looking for weekend flea markets. It took me a while to get back into the swing of things. After talking to some other full-time vendors, it wasn't too long before I got into the best markets.

Tie-dyes sold much better up north – profitable, but also highly demanding. I ramped up my production, making shirts all week long, which meant I could only sell on weekends. A small sports card section became a permanent part of my setup, and did very well. This led to discovering collectible card shows.

These specialized shows were held on various days throughout the week, almost always in New Jersey. At first I just saw them as a great source of product for the flea markets. Soon, however, I was doing these shows every day of the week.

With a baby on the way, I needed to stop making tie-dyes because the dye was toxic and unsafe for a child to be around. Since there was a seemingly unlimited amount of card shows and flea markets, I realized that if I stopped making shirts, there would be much more time to sell. Even though the profit margin was lower, selling cards all the time mean I could make more money overall.

Once I decided to focus on cards and comics full time, the change was pretty quick. I set up accounts with a comic book distributor so I could buy new issues at wholesale. I also started direct accounts with all the sports card manufacturers: Topps, Fleer, and Donruss, as well as Upper Deck, a new company that had just arrived on the scene.

And with that, I was doing card shows three or four nights a week, with flea markets on the weekends. I did better at the markets than the shows, but both were going quite well. If I got rained out on a weekend, I could usually squeeze into a show somewhere. I had a small black Toyota pickup truck that got decent gas mileage. Back then gas was still very cheap, so I could turn a profit even if I had to travel two hours to a show.

Now, I wasn't always the most competitive vendor of sports cards. At some of these shows there would be well-established businesses with massive setups. But I didn't only have cards. My comic book section was growing every day, and the comics boom was on the horizon.

I gained a reputation as "the comic guy" at the card shows. This encouraged me to specialize, and soon I was dragging a selection of superhero shirts, toys, and other merchandise with me everywhere I went.

Additionally, since baseball cards were the most popular and therefore the most saturated portion of the sports card market, I branched out into other sports. Basketball has always been my favorite sport, as I have been an active player and fan my whole life, so that is where I chose to specialize. By expanding into underrepresented markets, I was able to stand out from the rest of the card vendors.

Not only did this make me a decent living, but these shows also turned out to be a great means to acquire more product, as I had originally assessed. I made some of my best deals with fellow vendors. Some of them only did shows part time, or as a hobby. They would do one show a month or every few months, and didn't stay current on card values. As a full-time seller, I stayed up to date on prices and the hot new trends. Armed with that knowledge, I constantly looked out for items I could flip for a quick profit.

The best deals always happened before the doors opened to the public. I always arrived very early and set my table up immediately. Then I'd throw a tarp over it and walk around trying to find deals. I kept cash in my pocket and looked for people pricing things too low. It wasn't a very nice practice but that's how I survived. Card shows were a very cutthroat environment.

Then there were times when I had a show booked but was low on merchandise. I always had new comics, but those sales usually just covered the cost of the table, plus lunch and gas on a good day. On days when I had little to sell and a pocketful of cash, occasionally I'd try to buy out another vendor. I would go up to their table and ask, "How much for everything?" This worked a few times -- I cleaned them out before the show even started, and they went home to kick back and count their money. Usually, however, I just focused on buying up the hottest items.

When customers came to me trying to sell stuff, on the other hand, I could be quite brutal. For example, say someone came up to me trying to sell a card collection and I offered them $100. If they weren't satisfied with that price, they were free to go see if someone else would give them more. But if they came back, I'd only offer them $75. I never let my quoted price be used against me. Some people got furious and consider it an insult. I told them it was my best offer, and if they came back it would only be lower. Even so, plenty of those people still sold to me at the lower price.

Despite getting more than my share of good bargains, I also found plenty of bad ones at these shows and flea markets. I tried to keep my slate as clean as possible, but occasionally I got drawn into a bad deal. One of these began at a flea market called Rice's, held on Tuesdays in a big field in the middle of nowhere, Pennsylvania.

One morning an old lady stopped by my booth with a bunch of sports cards in a brown paper bag. I told her I didn't mind taking a look. To my surprise, this old lady had four Michael Jordan rookie cards, a couple of Mickey Mantle cards, and some other primo stuff in great condition! I had a somewhat limited budget, so just bought the four Michael Jordan rookies, paying her $600. At the time, the book price of a Jordan rookie was $900, and although they were realistically selling for half that amount at card shows, I still figured I could more than triple my money.

I was very happy with my deal -- until the next day when I found out they were counterfeits. In the tie-dye business this is not really something you have to deal with, especially if you're making the merchandise yourself. It would not be the last time I encountered counterfeit merchandise, so I learned an important lesson that day. I managed to sell them all to a dealer for $300, making it clear that they were counterfeits, so I recouped at least half of my money. I didn't ask what that dealer was going to do with them.

Between people trying to rip you off and those who will just outright try to steal your stuff, there are more than enough shady people to deal with. But some of the worst thieves are the ones who steal your most valuable product: time. Such was the case with Marge and Henry, a rather unpleasant elderly couple from Garfield, New Jersey. For several years, they attended almost every card show that was held in that state. I was never happy to see them.

Back then, smoking was still allowed at many of the shows, other than those held in hotels. Pretty much everywhere else, even in firehouses, people were smoking. You could smell Marge and Henry coming and see their cloud of smoke long before you saw them. Marge always had a lit cigarette in her mouth, and for Henry, a big cigar.

I often split a table with my friend Jeff. I met Jeff at one of the regular sports card shows that were then occurring every day of the week somewhere in New Jersey. He and I became friends, along with a few of the other regular vendors. We often bought multiple tables together in order to get a discount. We also watched tables for each other when one of us had to go to the bathroom.

Jeff was from Barnegat, a little town in south Jersey, where he also owned a modest baseball card shop. His dad, in his late seventies at the time, ran the store. I never saw Jeff or his dad without a New York Yankees baseball cap on their heads. Jeff had been a sports card seller from before the boom, and never dabbled outside his realm.

Jeff's dad kept the store while Jeff was out doing shows. While I enjoyed Jeff's company, and splitting tables with him was mutually beneficial, there was only one catch: Jeff's father was friends with Marge and Henry. This meant they were always hanging around our table. I had to deal with them and their smoke at show after show. I later found out that Jeff could not stand them either and only put up with them out of respect for his dad.

Marge and Henry would look around my setup all the time and occasionally try to buy something, but they always wanted it super cheap. I already had what were usually the lowest prices in the room, and I was willing to make deals on top of that for good customers. But Marge and Henry were not good customers. In the eight years that I knew them, I never sold one thing to them.

No price was ever low enough for them. No matter how I dropped it, they would still want a better deal. If I offered to sell them a dollar card for 75 cents, they would want it for 50 cents. Their favorite line was, "How much for me?" They were not the only ones to use that line, but my response to anyone who asked that question was always the same: a higher price. It was the same if someone said, "Could you do any better?" I'd quote them a higher price, and when they asked how that was better, I told them it was better for me.

Despite not getting along with Marge and Henry, I got roped into a partnership running a New Year's Day show with Marge at a hotel in Clark, NJ. She had the location and I could get the vendors. We did this for five years and it was a surprisingly well attended show. Although she always managed to cheat me out of some money, every year was still profitable enough for me to do it again.

After each week's Parsippany show Marge and Henry liked to head to Fuddruckers, a chain restaurant specializing in burgers. Jeff also loved that place, so I was dragged along with him, and we inevitably ran into them there. Fortunately, we always sat in the nonsmoking section, at a safe distance from them.

Fuddruckers had a self-service toppings bar for their burgers. Marge and Henry came prepared with large zip-top plastic bags that they stuffed full of onions, tomatoes, lettuce, and more. The worst was when Henry walked out of the restaurant toting an entire bag of whole onions, which had been displayed decoratively.

In addition to their vegetal thefts, I was quite sure they were also stealing cards from vendors at shows. Some dealers had long boxes full of single cards that they sold for a quarter each. Henry spent hours looking through these, and then only buy one card. Even though those were basic cards without much value, I am sure his pockets were just as stuffed with cards as those bags of lettuce and onions.

Eventually, Jeff grew so tired of Marge and Henry that he offered them $500 in cash to never again stop by his table at any show. Jeff was a very nice and polite guy but he had enough. They were appalled by the offer at first, but as I am sure you can surmise, they took the $500. I witnessed the cash being handed over to Henry. Due to my friendship with Jeff, I stopped doing the New Year's Day show with Marge, and that was the last I interacted with either of them.

One nice thing about selling to the Deadheads is that you never encountered people like this. It was a very carefree experience where customers were happy to pay full price for a quality tie-dye. If they asked for a deal it was because they really were too broke to afford the top rate.

But those days were over. When I finally decided to stop selling tie-dyes, I committed myself to a life of haggling and dealing with lunatics like Marge and Henry. In addition, I had to constantly monitor the values of the cards I was selling to make sure I was always getting the best possible price. Although making tie-dyes was very labor intensive, in many ways selling sports cards became an even more grueling lifestyle. But it did not matter to me, as long as the cash kept flowing in and I could pay my bills.

Chapter 6

For the next two years, I alternated between the Swap Shop in Florida during the winter, and card shows and flea markets up north the rest of the year. While sports cards remained a very popular item, this was when comic books began to really explode in popularity. When I returned to the Swap Shop in winter of 1991, they were already much more popular than the previous year, with several other vendors out there selling them.

There was one seller who was there every day with comics, so I figured he was doing well with them. One Thursday morning, I was talking to him when an old man came waddling up to his booth. The old man said he was looking for the comic book guy, and claimed to have a big stack of old comic books back at his setup. The so-called "comic book guy" declined to go look at them, stating that he had to take a dump, and might come by after that. I told the old man that I wouldn't mind taking a look. We walked over to his spot, which took about fifteen minutes because it was way out on the edge of the market. As we walked, the old man told me he wanted $100 for the stack of comics, with no option for negotiation.

When we finally arrived, the comics were there as promised. They were sitting in a pile on the ground, loose, with nothing protecting them. I flipped through and saw that they were all from the early 1960s. The first things of value I noticed were a few Gold Key *Star Trek* comics. But then I saw the crown jewel of the stack: *Amazing Fantasy* #15, the very first appearance of Spider-Man. The old man was very happy to make that sale, and a little surprised that I wanted them so badly!

That stack of comics wound up being very profitable for me. I sold the copy of *Amazing Fantasy* #15 for $900. It was in good condition, far from gem mint but still very rare to find. I recently saw one in similar condition sell for $17,000. That was in 2013. I sold mine in 1991, shortly after acquiring it, when the price guide said a gem mint copy was worth $8800. As copies of comics in good condition usually go for 10 percent of the top price, I was happy to get $900 for it. Even knowing that it has since sky-rocketed in price, I don't regret selling it when I did. It bought plenty of diapers for my infant son.

That winter I also discovered a comic book convention in West Palm Beach. I still had my box of valuable comics from the 60s which I had no luck with the year before. I figured that a dedicated show for comic books would be the best place to sell them. I had attended comic book conventions before as a fan, but this was going to be my first one as a vendor.

When I got to the show I was placed in a spot right next to one of the biggest dealers in the state, Tropic Comics. I was worried at first that it was impossible to compete with them, as their spot dwarfed mine. It happened to work out very well for me because I was able to make some great trades with the owner of Tropic Comics. The most notable was a high-grade copy of *Amazing Spider-Man #4* from 1963. It was valued at about $500 at the time, and I traded it for 100 copies of *Punisher #1*.

Punisher #1 was a brand new title. The Punisher was a character who originally debuted in 1973 as a villain in *Amazing Spider-Man #129*. He didn't appear again for several years, and then was reintroduced as an antihero in the 80s. He was a Vietnam veteran seeking vengeance against the mafiosos who had slaughtered his family. His methods were much more violent than the traditional Marvel heroes, and darker heroes were becoming all the rage.

Even more popular than the Punisher was Wolverine. He had been part of the X-Men for years and starred in his own four-issue solo miniseries written by Frank Miller in 1982. But it wasn't until the 90s, when he moved far beyond the X-Men and started appearing everywhere, that he truly peaked in popularity.

Then there was Ghost Rider, the spirit of vengeance, who rode a chopper-style motorcycle and beat his foes with chains. He had also been around for years, originally appearing in Western comics. Ghost Rider acquired his flaming skull, black leather jacket, and motorcycle in 1972, but it wasn't until 1990 when he was updated yet again that he really took off, joining the wave of similarly dark characters.

These three edgy and violent Marvel heroes were reaching unprecedented levels of popularity, and all their #1 issues were soaring in value. Those 100 *Punisher* #1's had a 75-cent cover price. They were selling for $5 apiece when I got that stack, and were going for $15 by the time I got back to New York.

Beyond their own books, *any* issue that the Punisher, Wolverine, or Ghost Rider appeared in became hot. They started making guest appearances in all Marvel's underselling titles, and for a while it worked. Marvel even made a special one-shot crossover book called *Hearts of Darkness* that featured all three of them together. It was called a "deluxe" issue and sold for five times the price of a regular issue. It was overhyped and overpriced, but sold well anyway, although not above the cover price.

Gimmicks like that took over the comic book industry for a while. A few early successes led to endless waves of imitators. One of the first big "special" issues that helped bring about the comics boom was *Ghost Rider* #15, featuring a glow-in-the-dark cover. This book received tons of hype outside the comic world, which was rare at the time. It had a $1.75 cover price, but people were willing to pay as much as $15 for it when it came out. What followed was a wave of not just glow-in-the-dark covers, but holographic, foldout, die-cut, chromium, and every kind of gimmick cover imaginable. So while *Ghost Rider* #15 did have a mind-blowingly cool cover, the novelty wore thin after what seemed like hundreds more glow-in-the-dark covers. After the new *X-Men* #1 had five different covers, *X-Force* #1 had to upstage it by having five different covers *and* five different trading cards, and so on and so forth. The impact on the comic book industry is still felt to this day.

Chapter 7

While no single issue or character created the comic book boom, perhaps the most important event was the formation of Image Comics. In an unprecedented move, all the most prominent artists working in the comics industry at that time decided to leave Marvel and DC, and start their own company.

These artists' names on the covers of comics guaranteed good sales, but they had grown frustrated with the ownership rights over the characters they worked on. Since Superman debuted in 1938, superheroes have always been property of the comic book company, not the writer or the artist. Tired of this practice, in 1992 the top talent struck out on their own.

Head among these rebellious artists was Todd McFarlane, who worked on various Spider-Man titles and was the first artist to draw Venom, perhaps Spider-Man's most iconic villain. McFarlane was paid a standard page rate for the issues featuring Venom's debut but received no royalties or rights to the character beyond that. Like Wolverine, Ghost Rider and the Punisher, Venom became one of the most desirable characters of the time, and Marvel started having him pop up in dozens of titles. McFarlane, along with several other top artists working for Marvel, decided to leave and create their own company with their own characters.

This bold move caused a media frenzy, and all Image's comics were hotly anticipated. Before the comic boom, ordering 25 copies of a single issue was considered a large order. I ordered at least 250 copies of all the first wave #1's. For McFarlane's title, *Spawn*, I ordered 1000.

I sold almost all of them at the cover price of $1.95. After bagging and boarding the issue, I made about 75 cents. While *Spawn* was a hot comic, the attention Image drew from general public who had not paid much attention to comics before was matched by just as many new sellers.

Sports card vendors started jumping into comics. Even those who never dabbled in comics before were buying up the Image titles in quantity. This led to too many copies of these issues floating around for them to really go much above cover price.

After several months, some of the #1's did rise in value. *Spawn* was by far the most lucrative, with many early issues holding value for a while. This was because it was generally agreed to be the best comic Image was putting out. The story was decent, and of course the art was fantastic. Like the popular Marvel heroes of the time, Spawn was a dark and violent antihero. So were most of the Image characters, but critics and readers soon found them to be all grit and no substance. All the artists tried to become writers too, and it wasn't always successful.

Most of Image's early titles had great art and terrible stories, with generic, bloodier counterparts of whatever the artist had been doing at Marvel. Rob Liefeld, who was popular for his work on X-Men spinoff comics like *X-Force*, launched several different books, including *Youngblood* and *Brigade*. They were basically X-Men rip offs with confusing stories and forgettable characters.

Jim Valentino's Image offering was *Shadowhawk*, another heavily-hyped first-wave book. *Shadowhawk* #1 had a silver-embossed cover and was very valuable for a short time, but quickly dropped in value as the story didn't hold interest.

While Image was a boon for the comic book industry in terms of distribution, with millions of copies of their early books being printed, I certainly didn't think it helped the quality of comic books themselves. For a while it seemed like you could only get a comic with good writing or good art, but not both.

Marvel and DC still had all the best writers, but the best artists in the industry had moved to Image. So while DC in particular had lots of good storylines going on, the art was usually mediocre. Meanwhile Image was cranking out eye candy with no substance.

Image's lack of good writing didn't matter all that much though, because most of the people buying their books didn't even read them. There was a whole wave of speculators who walked around at shows buying ten copies of every Image book but never read any of them. People saw how the comics from their own childhoods had risen in value, some selling for six figures, and thought they could do the same with these new books. It got to a point where most of the kids getting comics at the time were caught up in the same gamble, putting their comics away thinking they would get rich, instead of taking the time to enjoy them.

Of course this gold rush could not last. When I was a kid, comics did not have print runs in the millions, and hardly anyone thought to try to preserve them. They were considered disposable entertainment, so parents threw them out and kids tore them up or left them outside in the rain.

During the 90s comic boom, people were flocking to buy ten bagged and boarded copies of each issue and locking them away immediately. There was nothing rare about them, and the only people who actually wanted them just wanted to sell them. With no real demand, they quickly plummeted in value.

Each new Image release sold less than the issue before it. Every few months a new artist would come out with their own character, which meant a new #1, where the art was usually excellent but the story was always disappointing.

Another problem plaguing Image was that their comics never came out on time. Titles were supposed to appear every month, but three months often passed between issues of a given title. Without the tight infrastructure of editors and publishers that the big companies had, the inexperienced Image faltered.

With Image quickly slipping in popularity and being deeply discounted at card and comic shows, I decided to stop buying from them altogether. The sports card dealers were still ordering in huge quantities, so it certainly was the right move.

One title, Pitt, took so long to come out that despite ordering 250 copies of #1, I was entirely done with Image by the time it arrived. *Pitt* was the debut Image title by Dale Keown, famous for his work on *Incredible Hulk*. It came out nine months late, and by then all the other dealers had had a chance to increase their order quantity.

Pitt was expected to be a huge hit. The night after it came out, I did a show in Paramus, New Jersey, and I saw most dealers asking $5. I put mine out at cover price, $1.95. A dealer named Big Joe came up to me immediately and asked me how much for all of them. I told him the best I could do was $1.50 each, and he took all 250 copies I had. This was on a Thursday. The following Saturday I was at the Wayne Firehouse show, also in New Jersey, and saw he had a big stack of them out for sale at $1 each. That was when I knew the Image hype had truly come to the end.

Despite not living up to everyone's wild predictions, Image sold a lot of books and made a lot of money. They stumbled for a while, but still survive today. Some of the original titles are still going, most notably *Spawn* and *Savage Dragon*. Most of the original Image creators went back and worked for Marvel or DC at some point. Jim Lee, probably the second biggest artist at Image when it started, is now the chief creative officer at DC Comics.

Image has since taken on a new life, with plenty of successful titles in recent years. Their most successful current title is *The Walking Dead*, written by Robert Kirkman, who is the president of Image today. *The Walking Dead,* a black-and-white zombie comic, didn't make a huge impact when it came out. It grew in popularity until it was turned into a TV show, which was very successful and proved Image can still produce top tier comics. In terms of creator rights in the comics industry, Image certainly changed the status quo, so their story is ultimately a positive one even if their moment in the spotlight was short.

Chapter 8

Image was far from the only independent comic book company popping up in the 90s. Unlike Image, however, most did not last very long. There were a few that rivaled Image's popularity, most prominently Valiant Comics.

Valiant was actually founded in 1990, before Image, though it flew under the radar for the first year or so. The company was the brainchild of Jim Shooter and Bob Layton, who had formerly served as writers and editors at Marvel. For the first couple of years, they published rebooted versions of old Western Publishing characters like Magus, Robot Fighter and Doctor Solar, Man of the Atom but not many people even knew they were doing that.

It was not until the summer of 1992, the same time the first few Image #1's were appearing, that Valiant blew up. Earlier that year they had started publishing original titles, like *Harbinger*, *X-O Manowar*, and *Rai*. Then they had a storyline called, "Unity", a crossover that ran through all their titles and featured all their characters. The first part of the story, *Unity* #0, was given out for free. This generated a lot of interest and brought Valiant into the public eye. The story was eighteen parts in total and was a truly great epic saga.

Interest in Valiant grew. They had fresh and imaginative stories, which set them apart from Image and most of the other independent publishers. While the art wasn't nearly as flashy, they were publishing some of the best comic stories around at the time.

Then Jim Shooter released the numbers for the print runs of all the Valiant books prior to Unity. There were about fifty different issues across the various titles, all of which were printed in much smaller quantities than any of the Marvel, DC, or Image titles. This made them actually rare, not just temporarily selling at high prices because of hype and speculation.

Suddenly people were scrambling to find those early issues, and prices soared. All the Unity issues were also selling well above cover price, a craze within a craze. There were a couple of guys calling themselves the "Valiant Kings", who were buying anything Valiant had put out before Unity. I saw them at shows from Baltimore to New York, and they even cleaned me out a few times. On the other hand, I cleaned plenty of people out of their Valiant stuff too. However, nobody paid a higher price than the Valiant Kings.

I remember once at the Wayne Firehouse I bought a box full of Valiant comics from a regular comic book seller. It was before the show started, when he was setting up. He had about 20 boxes of comics, separated by company. When I asked him how much for the Valiant box, he told me $1000, take it or leave it. I happily agreed to take it. I moved the box to my table, leaving the issues with the prices he had put on them.

Throughout the show there was a feeding frenzy on that box, and I nearly doubled my money. The only bad part was that the guy I purchased the box from was set up right next to me, and he did not sell much during the show. He refused to deal with me ever again, but he sure was happy to take the $1000 at the time.

With the value of pre-Unity stuff rising every day, Valiant decided to capitalize on it. They introduced a gold logo program, where they published a limited edition of each issue with a gold embossed logo on it. A dealer received one gold logo book for every 100 regular issues they ordered. Soon dealers were ordering Valiant books by the thousands. People were paying around $100 for the gold logo versions, but the regular editions became completely worthless.

This ultimately killed Valiant. At card shows, dealers were trying to sell newly released Valiant issues for 25¢, when they had $2.25 cover price. The quality of the writing dropped too, as new titles were being churned out to try to capitalize on the Unity boom. None of it caught on, and soon even the gold logo versions were slipping in value. The whole thing crashed within a year.

Larry, a baseball card vendor, opened an account with Hero's World Distribution and over-ordered all the upcoming Valiant issues. He was not alone, and many card vendors had done the same exact thing. Most vendors ended up not taking their orders, losing their accounts with comic book distributors, and returning to sports cards. Larry, however, did take his full order.

Not even a year later, Larry asked me if I was interested in taking 50,000 Valiant books, split evenly between a dozen different titles, for free. He was tired of paying the storage fee to keep them and was offering them to anybody who would take them away. I declined his offer. Those Valiant books were so over-ordered, you can still find them for 25 cents in comic book stores now, over 25 years later.

Jim Shooter left Valiant in 1993 to start another comic company called Defiant. Their big comic was *Plasm* (later *Warriors of Plasm*), which had a very gimmicky start. Issue #0 was released in the form of trading cards. The whole thing was a puzzle that had to be assembled. The cards were sold by the pack, along with a limited-edition binder to hold the cards. This allowed collectors to assemble the set and read the cards as a comic book. There were also special insert cards, even going as far as to include cards autographed by Jim Shooter. Everything was well done, and it became extremely popular for a brief time.

People went crazy for these cards thinking they were the next big thing. At a show in Montclair, New Jersey, I sold every box of cards and every binder the night they were released. The boxes had a retail price of $45, but I sold them for $75. I had the lowest price in the room and easily sold all 36 boxes I had. I was also the only person in the room who had the binders, which flew off my table at $50 apiece. It was a great night but Defiant never recaptured that level of success.

By the time *Warriors of Plasm* #1 came out, the card boxes were selling for $20 and you could buy the full card set for $5. *Warriors of Plasm* #1 itself was only going for $1, less than half of the cover price, because everyone had ordered tons. I had a hundred and was lucky to sell them all for a dollar each, below my cost. Dealers who got stuck with them tried selling them for a quarter, or just threw them away. No one cared about Defiant again after that.

It didn't help that *Warriors of Plasm* #1 was delayed for three months by a lawsuit. Marvel said that Defiant's original title, *Plasm*, was too similar to a Marvel title called *Plasmer*. Defiant eventually won but the cost of the legal battle crippled them. After *Plasm* #0, the title had to be changed to *Warriors of Plasm*. This hurt their flagship title and none of their other comics took off.

Defiant quickly ceased publication. Issues that were solicited never hit the stands. The company had also just started a Unity-style crossover, which would have run across all the titles and brought all the Defiant characters into it. It was not enough to save them. Only the first two issues of that storyline were published. Defiant was never heard from again.

A big wave of independent comics featuring female heroes started in late 1992. The breakout book in this genre was *Vampirella* #1 by Harris

Comics. This was a reboot of an old black-and-white comic book with the same title, but this time in full color. When I was growing up I always read plenty of horror comics like *Creepy*, *Eerie*, and *Weird*, so I was familiar with the character. I had a feeling it was going to be a hit so I ordered 50 copies.

The night *Vampirella* #1 came out, I was at LT's Golf Club doing a show that was mostly sports cards. It was in New Jersey, right next to Giants Stadium where I used to sell tie-dyed gloves. Another dealer bought the entire stack, giving me $200 for the 50 copies. I was happy to have doubled my money.

Unfortunately for me, *Vampirella* #1 was selling for $50 each a few weeks later. I knew they were going to be good; I did not know they were going to be that good.

After the success of *Vampirella*, other independent companies followed suit and began releasing similar books. Not wanting to miss another opportunity, I kept a close eye on the independent female heroes. The next hot title in this genre was *Lady Death* #1. It had a chrome cover and I knew it would be a big seller. The cover price was $3.50, very high for that time, but I took a chance and ordered 200 copies.

As it turned out, *Lady Death* #1 was heavily delayed, coming out a couple months late. I was worried that the hype for the title had died down and hesitated to put them out for too much. I was doing a show at the Middlesex Mall in New Jersey that week, and priced them at $5 each. By the end of the weekend I only had twenty copies left. I held onto those for a while, eventually letting them go for $25 each. The price continued to climb after that, topping out at $60.

After the popularity of those first two titles, a wave of imitators followed. Some, like *Shi*, were hits, but most tanked. Only the first issues were worth anything, even for *Vampirella* and *Lady Death*.

Then Marvel and DC caught on and started featuring their female characters more prominently. This meant female heroes became more common overall, though none hit as big as those first two. The craze quickly fizzled, but titles like *Vampirella* and *Lady Death* still pop up regularly today., with varying success. Regardless of how popular they were back then, the door was opened for more female heros and there are more today than ever before.

Chapter 9

DC Comics entered the 90s on a strong note, riding high on the success of Tim Burton's *Batman* in 1989. While this brought renewed interest in their comic books, it wasn't until 1992 that DC really stepped to the forefront of the industry. And to do it they only had to kill their biggest character.

"The Death of Superman" storyline ran from 1992 to 1993, through all the Superman-related titles published at the time. It was a very simple story. A mysterious alien killing machine, Doomsday, escapes his captivity inside the Earth and rampages across the country. He wrecks everything in his way, including the Justice League of America, who were helpless to stop him. Nothing even gives Doomsday pause until he arrives in Metropolis, where Superman is ready for him. The two behemoths go at it in a long and bloody battle. With no other means of beating the creature, Superman makes the ultimate sacrifice. The two collide at full force, seemingly killing both.

This story created a huge buzz in the media. A few years earlier, DC had killed off Jason Todd, who was Robin, Batman's sidekick, at that time. The decision to kill him or not was decided through a poll in newspapers where fans could vote on his fate. That campaign was quite successful in its own right, but it was still unheard of for a timeless hero like Superman to die.

All issues in the storyline quickly picked up in value. At first, people didn't realize that the *Justice League of America* issues were part of the story, so suddenly everyone was scrambling to find them. Of course, the most desirable and valuable issue of all was the one containing the actual death.

Superman #75 was the hot comic in the summer of 1993. While it could be found in bookstores and other places across the country, that was only the "newsstand" version. For specialized comic dealers like me, there was a special "hobby" edition in a black plastic bag printed with a Superman logo dripping blood. Inside the bag was the issue itself, along with a collector card and a black armband. Even more extravagant was a special platinum-colored bag holding an even rarer special edition. The platinum version was only offered to dealers who ordered #75 in large quantities.

This phenomenon was so big that every version of *Superman #75* flew off the shelves. I went around to bookstores buying them out of the newsstand version at the $1.25 cover price, having no problem selling them for $5. The black-bagged version had a $2.50 cover price and reached as high as $50 in comic book stores, though I was happy flipping them at $25 apiece. I sold my platinum-bagged version for $200 and was able to buy and sell a few more copies at the same price. "The Death of Superman" was huge, and everybody wanted a piece.

Lots of people who normally didn't care about comics at all were suddenly looking for

Superman #75. One of these was a guy named Johnny, a sports card collector in his late 40s. I saw him at all the big shows in northeastern New Jersey. Johnny never spent more than $10 on anything and always asked for a deal. If he was buying cards that cost $1, he would want three for $2, or two for a dollar and some change. Since he was usually after cheap stuff that didn't sell that well, I always took whatever deal he proposed. Until "The Death of Superman", that is.

Though he had never even looked at a comic before, Johnny desperately wanted that black-bagged version of #75. This was right at the peak of the frenzy. Word had spread that a Japanese businessman paid $200 for a copy on the street in Manhattan. The lowest I could be talked down to at the time was $22.

Johnny's best offer was $15. I refused him many times, always telling him I would gladly buy hundreds for $15 each if I could. Weeks went by and he tried to get every dealer he could to give him one for $15. Nobody accepted it, of course. I finally offered him one for $20 but he still wouldn't buy it.

One morning as I was heading to a show at the Holiday Inn in Totowa, New Jersey, it started snowing. It was unseasonable but not too heavy. I decided to push on, driving slowly because the road was getting slippery. I stopped to get some coffee, but soon my stomach started hurting, probably from the chopped meat and corn mixture I had eaten for dinner the night before. I didn't want to be late for the show, so I forged onward.

The snow and my stomach rapidly worsened. After a few minutes I was almost doubled over with pain. I felt really bloated and sat up to let out a fart. The fart brought a split-second of relief -- then a huge load of poop followed.

I had to keep driving with the mess in my pants for a few more miles until I saw a gas station. I was able to use my undershirt to clean up somewhat in the restroom, ridding myself of my underwear. But I had no choice but to put the soiled pants back on and head over to the show, assuming that I could grab a fresh pair at the K-Mart next to the location. Unfortunately, the store didn't open until the same time the show started. I was screwed.

I had prepaid $150 for the table at the show and had just forged through a small blizzard to get there, so I started setting up as usual. As the show began, I heard some customers complaining about the smell. I blamed it on the dealer next to me, who was overpriced and always arguing with the customers. Since the snow stopped, the show became very busy. I tried bribing a couple of people I knew to go over to K-Mart but everyone refused.

Then Johnny came to my table. I sighed with relief, figuring if anyone would make a deal to go get me a pair of sweatpants, it would be him. I told him I'll pay for the sweatpants and give him a free black-bagged *Superman #75* just for walking next door. But he wouldn't do it! Even though I had not told him why I wanted the sweatpants, I was stunned that he turned me down.

I suffered through the rest of the show, smelling quite awful in my nasty pants, and got a new pair immediately afterwards. I made over $300 in profit that day, one of my best shows. After that, I always kept an extra pair of sweatpants in my truck, I never drank coffee again, and Johnny never got *Superman #75*, at least not from me.

"The Death of Superman" was followed by the "Funeral For a Friend" storyline that ran through almost every DC title, showing the rest of the DC universe reacting to his death. Next, they introduced four new characters, all vying for Superman's place. There was a cyborg insisting he was the real Superman, another guy claiming to be from the future, then a younger, alternate-universe version of Superman. But the most famous, or rather infamous, of the new Supermen was none other than Steel.

Steel wore heavy armor alongside his red Superman cape and he wielded a massive hammer. He became the most recognizable face from the new crop of Supermen, thanks in part to a movie starring Shaquille O'Neal, known simply as Shaq to most. Shaq had been a massive basketball star before dipping into acting. Coincidently, there was a period of time in 1992 and 1993 when Shaq's rookie card was about equally as popular as *Superman #75*. Perhaps that is why he was chosen to star in a movie about Superman's replacement.

After the "Reign of the Supermen", the real Superman finally returned about a year later, with "The Return of Superman" special issue arriving in a white bag. All of the "Funeral for a Friend" and replacement Superman comics leading up to the return sold very well, but not for much above cover. I was able to move through the 25 copies of each I ordered. I thought that his return would generate huge interest, at least at first. I was tempted to order 5000 copies, but settled on 500.

I was fortunate that my comic book distributor was halfway between my apartment and the town of Parsippany, where I did a show every Tuesday night. New comics were shipped to dealers on Wednesdays, but when "The Return of Superman" was due, I stopped by Heroes World Distribution on my way to the Parsippany show and made a deal to get them that night.

Since I was the only one at that show who had "The Return of Superman" I quickly sold out of white-bagged copies. Thanks to my stop, I arrived over an hour late and couldn't get a table. Despite this, I paid the show promoter $50, the price of a table, and simply wheeled in my loaded hand truck, announcing "Superman is here!" The issue had a $2.95 cover price, so at $3 each and ten for $25, I sold all 500 copies within an hour.

"The Return of Superman" was not well received as a story. Fans felt that Superman had not been gone long enough, and the explanation for how he survived was poor. In addition, it was heavily over-ordered. After seeing how well I did with them that first night, a fellow vendor named Joey called Hero's World Distribution to raise his order from 1,000 copies to 10,000. At his cost of 50% off cover price, he was paying $1.49 an issue. By the next day, all the dealers had them in huge stacks. In the end, Joey sold the whole pallet of 10,000 to a dollar store chain for .25¢ each.

"The Death of Superman" was a great promotional event and created huge interest in the comic book world. But Superman's reign as the most popular superhero did not last too long, and many of the new fans brought in by headlines about his death dispersed soon after he returned. However, Superman was not the only DC hero with a storyline that gained national attention in the 90s.

Chapter 10

Following the smashing success of "The Death of Superman", DC put Batman in similar peril later in 1993. The "Knightfall" storyline ran through all of the Batman-related comics for four months and 60 issues, plus countless other tie-ins. The gist of the story was that Bane, a new villain, pitted all of Batman's classic foes against him, one after another. Only then, when Batman was at his weakest, did Bane reveal himself. Bane ended their battle by breaking Batman's back.

"The Breaking of the Bat" was highly anticipated. Everyone knew something big was coming, but not when it would go down. When you order wholesale comic books from a distributor, you place your order two months in advance. You are always calculating how many copies of an issue to buy in order to have enough of something big -- without being stuck with lots of copies of a dud. Fortunately, I knew a comic vendor named Pete who gave me an inside tip.

Pete was a chain smoker with greasy long hair and brown teeth. He still lived in his parent's basement at age 37. There were no windows down there, just a bed, a chair, and hundreds of boxes of comics. The floor was ankle deep in Budweiser cans and cigarette butts.

Despite his foulness, he was friends with some comic book writers and artists. He ran a monthly show in Philadelphia and always had his famous friends there. It was a little out of the way for me, but during the boom his shows always drew huge crowds, so I went to a few. During one of these shows he confided a tip about the "The Breaking of the Bat".

He told me it would happen in part 11 of the story, *Batman #497*. I asked him how many copies he planned to order. He told me he was getting 20 copies of each of the 60 parts, creating 20 full sets to sell. When I asked him why he didn't order more of *Batman #497*, he said, "Do you really think it will be worth more?" I said that if his information was correct, it definitely would be. I decided to take a chance.

At this point the eighth part of "Knightfall" had just come out. The first couple "Knightfall" issues were selling for $5, while the rest were only going for about a dollar. All the issues had a $1.25 cover price. Normally, the most I ordered of any of the "Knightfall" issues was 50 copies. For Batman #497, I ordered a thousand. Fortunately, Pete's tip was accurate. I was able to sell out in a few weeks, flipping them at $5 each.

Batman #497 eventually rose to around $10 and drove interest towards the "Knightfall" storyline. A relatively new Batman ally named Azrael took over as Batman for a while, quickly becoming psychotic with power. Ultimately, the two Batmen clashed and the original reclaimed the mantle, kicking Bane out of Gotham along the way. It was a great story, but none of the issues after the "The

Breaking of the Bat" sold for more than cover price. Dealers began ordering more, hoping for a repeat of Batman #497, but there never was one.

DC released a second printing of that issue a couple months later, quickly dropping the value back down to $5. After "The Death of Superman" and "Knightfall", DC didn't have another big hit for the rest of the decade. While the hype surrounding these events was short lived, both "The Death of Superman" and "Knightfall" are both remembered as classic stories that are still often reprinted and read by countless fans today!

Chapter 11

Collecting had become a craze. Sports cards and comics, once mere entertainment, were being hoarded by adults as well as children. This mania spread to just about every kind of entertainment for kids. When something became popular, every kid in America wanted it and their parents were willing to pay any cost to satisfy their crying children's demands. Nothing proved this point more than the arrival of the Power Rangers in 1993.

The Power Rangers were a group of costumed teenagers who battled monsters from outer space. The phenomenon began as a Japanese show for kids. Creators for the American version used the same characters and costumes to film scenes in English with American actors, then used those to frame the original Japanese fight scenes. Kids loved it.

When toy company Bandai introduced Power Rangers action figures, every kid had to have them. The original wave of Power Rangers figures was not nearly large enough to meet the demand. On top of that, Bandai had manufactured lower amounts of the two female figures, the Pink Ranger and the Yellow Ranger. This skyrocketed their value on the secondary market. Those two were going for quadruple the retail price, while the rest were selling for around double. Even more in demand, however, was the Megazord.

Megazord was composed of five individual Dinozords, one for each Power Ranger. These vehicles combined to make one large robot. It was an elaborate set, decadently expensive, and they flew off the toy store shelves. It was the ultimate Power Rangers figure, until the Dragonzord came along. The Dragonzord had the same shtick but was even more desirable because it came with the rare Green Ranger figure.

All the Power Rangers figures were hot at first and the demand was incredible. Customers were asking me for these before they were even released. To acquire these Power Rangers figures I was driven to a new source of merchandise I had never considered: retail stores.

The answer seemed obvious once I hit on it, and I was soon on a constant search for stores that had not sold out yet. In those days there were many others like myself, combing big box stores for resale items like the Power Ranger toys. I used to run into many middle-aged men in the toy aisles of stores throughout New Jersey and beyond. I spent most of my weekday mornings in that same aisle, trying to stock up as much as humanly possible before the weekend.

One Friday morning I was in K-Mart, at a shopping center where I never had much success. Since it was on my route I always diligently stopped by, though I was not expecting much. When I got to the toy section I thought I was hallucinating. There was an entire row of Power Ranger toys, including two Megazords! Each wholesale case only contained two Megazords so this store must have just put out their entire stock.

I immediately loaded up a shopping cart with as much as I could fit and got on line to pay. A lady approached me and scolded me for taking everything, so I offered to let her take whatever she wanted from my cart. She declined to take anything and just kept yelling and complaining to the cashiers while they were ringing me up.

When I arrived at the Chester Flea Market that Sunday, I filled two six-foot tables with the Power Rangers toys I picked up at K-Mart and started setting up the rest of my booth. The toys were a magnet for kids and they began flocking over. I did not finish setting up the rest of my booth until about four hours later. By that point I had sold over $2000 worth of Power Rangers toys, walking away with over $800 in profit.

A couple of weeks later, again at the Chester Flea Market, I noticed a t-shirt vendor who was selling child-sized Power Rangers shirts and hats. I was able to buy all he had left at the end of the day by promising not to sell them at the same market. Since they were bootlegs I was able to get the shirts for $2 and the hats for $1.50 each. I sold these everywhere I went, including baseball card shows, and they flew off my table at $5 apiece. I did business with that vendor for years. I always had shirts based on the brands I sold. I simply brought him designs and the next week he had the shirts.

Power Rangers exploded onto TVs then into toy stores worldwide, cementing their place in the children's entertainment industry. New versions of the show brought endless variations of the figures, though none caught on as much as that first wave. Soon the Power Rangers appeared on lunchboxes, posters, quilts, and just about everything imaginable. One item that featured images of the Power Rangers was another short-lived craze of the 90s: pogs.

The game that became known as pogs has been played in Hawaii since the 1920s. It was originally played with round milk caps, but by 1993 companies were producing special laminated discs for the sole purpose of gaming.

To play, you threw heavier plastic or metal discs called "slammers" at a stack of pogs. Any pogs that flipped over were worth a point each. Players put their own pogs in the stack, and you kept the ones you flipped over. It was a bit like gambling for kids -- and like any form of gambling, it was addictive.

A Hawaiian school teacher started using milk caps as part of her lesson plan in 1991. By 1993, milk caps had become pogs and spread across America. Kids went crazy for both playing the game and collecting them. They were cheap to produce, and very quickly just about every company out there was pumping out their own pogs.

You could buy some by the package, like trading cards, and collect others from things like cereal boxes. There were pogs featuring sports stars, movie and comic book characters, and yes, even the Power Rangers. McDonald's started giving out pogs with kids' meals, and every other fast food restaurant followed. You could even get exclusive pogs at Disneyland.

One day at a flea market, a kid confided his strategy to me as he purchased a slammer. He said that he was the smartest one, investing in slammers, not pogs, because the slammers would be worth the most in the future. Unfortunately, his prediction did not come true.

The pogs fad ended as quickly as it arrived, and neither pogs nor slammers held their value. Pogs that had sold for $5 a dozen weren't worth $5 for a thousand within a few months. It didn't help that many schools had banned pogs because they were too much of a distraction, and also because of the gambling element.

When pogs died, they died. Within a year of the peak of their popularity it seemed like kids had abandoned playing and collecting them entirely. For my part, I had avoided digging too far into it. I mostly acted as a sort of wholesaler to stores in my area. I sold pogs to them by the the case and box, though I did get involved in selling smaller quantities at flea markets.

In the end, I got stuck with a few thousand pogs, some loose and some in sealed packages. In the end, I put the pogs out for free and had many people happily take them, including my son James.

Chapter 12

In 1993, sports cards were still going strong, comics were hotter than ever, and new crazes were popping up all the time. Then a new type of product hit the market unlike any before. It was a twist on collectible cards but, unlike the ones you just looked at and put in a binder, these had another use as well.

This was the first trading card game, *Magic: The Gathering*. While card games like poker have been around for centuries, this put a spin on things by having customizable decks. To play, each participant needs at least sixty cards in their deck (though there are variants that use decks of different sizes), and there are tons of cards to choose from. The original series had a few hundred cards, and 25 years on, there are now over 10,000 unique *Magic* cards. Like sports cards, some are rarer and more expensive than others. And that variety is what drives the game.

I first heard about *Magic: The Gathering* shortly after it came out. One day in the fall of 1993, two different people came up to me at the Chester Flea Market to ask about the game. When someone asks me for something I don't have, I might consider it as a product. But two people asking on the same day warranted immediate investigation.

As soon as I looked into it, I knew I was onto something good. None of the comic book or sports card distributors were carrying *Magic* cards yet, so it took me all day to find out where to get them.

Eventually I found two distributors. One was large and sold all kinds of games and the other one was new and sold only Magic. I put in large orders with both.

The next week at Chester Flea Market marked the beginning of my time selling *Magic: The Gathering*. The products I received were from the *Unlimited* edition, following smaller *Alpha* and *Beta* editions. At that time there were just two types of products: starter decks and booster packs. The starter decks were the only way to get the rulebook, so they sold well, as did the booster packs. The cards featured beautiful artwork, and in the beginning many people bought them and didn't even play the game, just collecting them like other cards. There are still plenty of dedicated collectors today, but the idea of this new, customizable type of game is what turned *Magic* into a whole different phenomenon.

This was the birth of the trading card game. While countless imitators have followed, *Magic* was the first, and all its successors use some variant of the same basic of rules. In *Magic*, the idea is that you are a Wizard in a duel. Your deck is filled with spells and creatures to help you fight your opponent. Each player starts with twenty life points, and when you hit zero you lose. Different types of cards represent creatures like dragons, or spells such as lightning bolts, or artifacts like swords.

Then there are land cards, which produce mana, a resource you need to play your spells and creatures. Some cards require more mana than others, and you also have to have the right kind of mana, which comes in five different colors. White, blue, black, red, and green cards each have their own unique qualities and iconic creatures. The colors can also be combined, and some cards require multiple types of mana. This format allows for an infinite amount of possible cards, with hundreds of new ones coming out each year.

Magic only had a small following at first, but at that time I was the only one who had it at the flea markets and card shows in my area, so I did well. I learned how the game worked, since kids were always asking me how to play. I originally just did this as a way to sell more cards, but I quickly fell in love with the game itself.

At its core, *Magic* is a card version of the classic roleplaying game, *Dungeons and Dragons*. Many of the creatures and spells in early sets were borrowed directly from *D&D*. I had played *D&D* a little bit over the years but never really got into it. *Magic* was easier to learn, quicker to play, and, in my opinion, much more exciting. Being an active player helped me understand the game and sell it better for years, and I continue to play it today.

The first *Magic* expansion, *Arabian Nights*, came out in December of 1993. For the first time there was a new set of cards to add to existing decks. The buzz also brought in a whole bunch of new players. Demand for this set was much higher than anyone expected, and supplies were short. I had ordered a full case from each distributor, and each case normally had ten boxes. I only got a single box from one distributor, while the other sent me half a box worth of packs. While I was frustrated with being cut short, I learned not to make that mistake again. If anything, the release of *Arabian Nights* just showed the world that *Magic* was here to stay.

I was not able to get more *Magic* until April of 1994, when they released the *Revised* edition. This was another version of the original set, bringing back most of the cards from *Unlimited* except a select few. The most famous cards cut from the *Unlimited* set became known as the Power 9.

Wizards of the Coast, the company that produced *Magic,* decided to cut these because they were too powerful, and leaving them out of the new set would make for a more balanced game overall. But because players could still use these game breaking cards in their decks, the Power 9 instantly shot up in value.

Soon players were scrambling to get the Power 9, driving up the prices of the pre-*Revised* editions. I didn't know about this key difference between *Unlimited* and *Revised* at first, but learned quickly. I started traveling around New York, New Jersey, and even Pennsylvania, searching for gaming stores that still unknowingly had the *Unlimited* version.

I spent an entire week searching and was only able to round up 60 packs. I immediately opened them all to sell the cards individually. There were no established prices or official price guides at that point, so I used my knowledge of the game to price them out. I knew the Power 9 were worth more so I put them out at what I thought were high prices.

The highest-priced card was Black Lotus. I was shocked when I was able to get $40 for it. Black Lotus is the centerpiece of the Power 9, and certainly the most iconic *Magic* card of all time. While it doesn't do anything too incredible, giving a player three extra mana, it is extremely powerful and still used in certain tournaments that allow it today. And while it was a highly desirable card from the start, I don't think anyone back then could have predicted the value it would have over two decades later. These days a mint condition Black Lotus from *Alpha* can sell for as much as $100,000. That's a lot of money for a little piece of cardboard!

What was great about cracking open packs and selling the cards individually was that *everything* sold, for a little while at least. Each card was one of three rarities, and each had a different value. Commons sold for a quarter, lands for a dime. Uncommons were $1 and rares went for $3 and up.

The hot cards from *Revised* were Shivan Dragon which sold for $12, Lord of the Pit and Force of Nature which each went for $10, and the dual lands sold for between $5 to $8 apiece. Packs and boxes still sold well, but singles really took off for me. One day at the end of May 1994, I sat down and opened ten boxes of *Revised* packs, my headlong dive into selling *Magic* by the card.

This approach put me well ahead of the curve. Other dealers had caught on to *Magic*, but I was one of the first to sell singles. I could almost name my own price, since there were still no price guides yet.

Simply put, a card's value was whatever someone was willing to pay for it. Sometimes I was too high, other times too low, but overall I was making more money than I did selling the sealed packs and boxes. Prices on single cards stabilized once *InQuest*, a magazine catering to collectible card gamers, began publishing price guides in 1995.

In February of 1994 a *Magic: The Gathering* convention was held in Philadelphia. There was a big tournament with *Magic* boxes for prizes, and about 50 dealer tables. This was one of the first big *Magic* tournaments and a totally new concept to me.

That was not the only new thing for me that night, as I had just received a huge order of the *Star Trek* collectible card game. This was part of the first wave of *Magic* imitators, all trying to replicate the overnight success of *Magic*. I over ordered *Star Trek*, thinking I'd only get a fraction of my order as had happened with the *Magic* cards. Surprisingly, I did get everything I ordered, and brought the whole load to the *Magic* convention in Philly.

The show was far more popular than I expected. I lived about four hours away and had not been able to get a hotel room for the night before. I was lucky to run into a vendor I knew and was able to share a room. We played the sealed deck format of *Magic* for keeps in the room, which gave us both extra cards to sell at the show the next day.

At the show itself, *Magic* was great but the *Star Trek* card game was even better for me. I sold out at $90 a box, the full retail price. Then I took all that money and went to a dealer who had piles of all the expensive *Magic* cards. He was selling Black Lotus for $75, not a bad price at the time. I went home with six of those, plus dozens of other big money cards. After that I raised my price on Black Lotus to $125. Within two weeks I had sold out of everything I bought in Philadelphia.

Between *Magic*, sports cards, and comics, my business was growing almost unmanageable. While I was raking in some cash, I was spending most of my time on the road. At shows and flea markets people kept asking me if I had a store. That seemed like an impossible dream for those first couple of years of vending. But when *Magic* exploded, I decided it was doable after all. A month after that convention in Philadelphia, helped greatly by the profit I made off that show, I opened my store.

Chapter 13

I had been keeping my eye out for an available store for a while and by the time it happened I had looked high and low. I even considered trying to open a store in Florida when I was down there. Eventually I found the perfect spot in Hackettstown, New Jersey. I discovered it on the way to a show one day. It was halfway between all the major card shows and flea markets I was doing at the time, so it was perfectly located. Even better, the rent was low.

The space that was to become my store began as a one-bedroom apartment that the landlord was willing to convert. The rent was $400 a month. It wasn't a huge space, only 600 square feet, but it did have a bathroom and a huge porch. An eight-foot table at a mall show cost $150, and the weekly Tuesday show in Parsippany cost $50, so what I was paying for the store was comparatively a bargain. I moved to an apartment in Netcong, a nearby town, and the store was ready two weeks later.

For the name, I chose "Collectibles: Cards, Games, and Comics." For one thing, it is very easy for people to see what type of store it is. More importantly, it was cheaper to advertise. Back before the convenience of the internet, people used the yellow pages in the phone book to find businesses. When you created your listing, you paid by the word for the business description – but the name of the business itself was free. Embedding my store's description in its name saved me on advertising, which was important because I had very limited funds to open the store.

I never took any loans to cover the rent or pay for inventory. I stocked the store with what I had, and advertised in the cheapest ways possible. For example, I bought three orange cones and taped big arrow signs on them, directing people to my store. I did that for about a year, bringing them in at the end of each night. I also had a huge 6' x 3' sign that faced the road. Between the sign and the cones, I was able to attract curious customers.

Since I had been a cash-only business for years, I didn't have a credit card machine when I opened – actually, I didn't even have a cash register! In 1994 you could get away with that. I just used a notebook to record my sales for the first few months until I could afford a cash register. It was nearly a year before I finally got a credit card machine. I never had an actual credit card of my own until the next millennium.

The store opened on March 1st, 1994. I had a show booked at the Middlesex Mall that weekend, so I wasn't even able to attend the opening myself. The Middlesex Mall was one of my best shows, so I had to divide my merchandise carefully, making sure not to leave too much at the store. The store did decent business that opening weekend even with the bare spots in the displays.

This changed quickly. First, I pinned up bagged and boarded comics all over the walls. They were the comics I did not need at flea markets and shows, mostly superhero stuff from the 60s and 70s. I priced them at half the guide book price. They didn't sell too well but were great for decoration. I also had a few dollar boxes filled with comic books, plus a couple of racks of new issues.

Everything else was on folding tables. I had about a dozen boxes of sports card packs, both current and old. I had always had an interest in collecting rock music memorabilia, so I put all that out as well. Other than that, the only other thing I sold was *Magic: The Gathering*.

My *Magic* selection wasn't huge at first, but grew quickly. I had *Revised* starters and boosters, and always kept plenty of the most recent set on hand, along with a big selection of older sets. I also had a jewelry case filled with singles. Next to that were the bins of common and uncommon cards. Finally, I put some tables and chairs in the back so customers could play *Magic*.

When I first opened my store, there was already both a baseball card shop and a comic book shop in Hackettstown. Neither one of them carried *Magic*, so that was my best seller right out of the gate. Several kids told me they had asked the other stores to carry it but those owners decided not to. Once word spread, kids poured into my place. After that the tables in the back were never empty.

When I was around during the week, I was always teaching new kids how to play. Soon I started selling beginner decks that I made myself, which sold for $5. This was a very popular item and got people into the game. Then I decided to start a *Magic* tournament.

Every Thursday afternoon at 4:30, my store filled up with players of all ages for the weekly *Magic* tournament. This was well before Wizards of the Coast started offering sanctioned tournaments and providing prize support to store owners. Eventually they started these on Friday nights, and even little stores like mine could participate. But I chose Thursday night because I needed Friday to divide up merchandise and pack for the weekend. I chose 4:30 so kids could play when they got out of school.

When Wizards introduced the Friday night events, I stuck with Thursday. That left me out of their prize support but I had been doing that just fine on my own. Since everyone at my store was already used to Thursdays, it didn't affect my tournaments much and they continued to be well attended for years.

As word of mouth spread, more players popped up. Kids would get their friends to play. In a small town in New Jersey there wasn't much for kids to do besides playing sports, so I felt that offering these tournaments was good for the community.

One day, a 14-year-old kid named Craig came into my store sometimes to buy baseball cards. He badly wanted a Ken Griffey Jr. Upper Deck rookie card. I picked one up at a show for him. Although I paid $45 for it, I sold it to him for just $50 when he said that was the most he could afford. The card had a $80 book price and was very desirable at that time. After that he began to come to the store more frequently.

I noticed Craig was interested in *Magic* cards, so I taught him the game one day. He came back the next week and bought a deck plus a bunch of singles. Soon he was playing in the tournaments. He was having a lot of fun but his mom didn't like the cards, thinking they might be demonic.

The Satanic panic that began in the 1980s still lingered, and the cards had gotten a bit of bad press because demons were printed on black cards, the color that usually represents evil characters in the game. Demons briefly stopped appearing in the game and one card called Unholy Strength had to be reprinted without a pentagram.

While these worrisome aspects were certainly part of the game, they were not the focus. I explained this to Craig's mom, pointing out that it is really just a strategy game that the smarter kids played. Several of his peers were also into it, so she could see it was harmless fun. Though she wasn't thrilled, she allowed him play.

Craig became a very good player. He soon became friends with Jon, who was probably the best *Magic* player in the store. Jon was five years older than Craig and came from a town twenty minutes away. He was a little eccentric, always shuffling his deck exactly 21 times before every game.

Jon, like most other *Magic* players who bought lots of boxes over the years, accumulated thousands of common and uncommon cards he didn't need. I'd buy those cards in bulk at $25 for a box of 5000. I then repackaged these into 100-card assortments that new players loved. The interesting thing about the boxes I bought from Jon is that they were all alphabetized and sorted by color. I can't begin to imagine how long it would take to alphabetize 10,000 cards.

Jon was such a good player that I had to run a second tournament because of him. People kept calling the store to ask if Jon was playing. If he was, they wouldn't come because they knew they had little chance of winning. So I added a Thursday tournament at 3 PM for kids age 13 and under, and pushed the all-ages tournament back to 6 PM.

Splitting up the tournaments worked out well because I could have more total players in one night. Following the official tournaments, there were special after-hours games. These were always in what is known as limited formats, where you use sealed packs to make decks rather than bringing a deck you built previously. The stakes were much higher in these games, with all the cards going to the winner. I played in these games myself because they were truly fun.

During these after-hours games, the store stayed open, sometimes past midnight. I often got additional business in those extra hours. One night a well-dressed woman came in and was shocked to see the scene in the back. I told her if she needed anything to let me know. As she started looking around, I instructed the other players to watch their language. To my surprise she spent almost $300!

On another one of these late nights, a big tractor-trailer pulled into the parking lot around 11 PM. The driver had seen that I was still open. He came in, bought a 1982 Joe Montana rookie card and a box of Topps Football and went on his way. The card sold for $200 and the box was $40. I usually sold my best cards at shows, but when I was home I'd throw them in a case in the store. Usually it was pointless, but not that night.

The longer those *Magic* games went on, the more money I pulled in. Not only were they profitable, I also got to meet many cool people this way. One night I watched a kid lose a big prize pool. I had never seen him in the store before, and I critiqued his play to him after the game.

His name was John Finkel, and a year later he became the *Magic* World Champion. Wizards of the Coast issued a special deck that recreated John Finkel's winning deck. While I had criticized his play before, I did not hesitate to sell his championship deck, proudly telling customers that he had played *Magic* in my store not a year before.

Most of the *Magic* players I have met in my lifetime have been cool and friendly people. But as with any scene, there are always a few unsavory characters. I met one of the worst early on. At 6'5" tall and weighing in at over 300 pounds, he truly deserved the name Big Dave.

My store was small, and it was hard to squeeze Big Dave into a tournament, literally. But Big Dave was a big spender, buying several boxes of *Magic* from me upon each set's release. He had a high-paying job in the computer field. He always arrived with a huge duffel bag filled with *Magic* decks. He had at least 50 decks, and their average value at that time was about $500 per deck.

Like most older people, Big Dave was not a great *Magic* player. He just had all the good cards. All his decks were stuffed with the Power 9 and other expensive *Magic* cards. He would get really angry at the tournaments because little kids were continually beating him. Eventually it got to be too much for him and he resorted to cheating.

After catching Big Dave cheating several times, I eventually banned him from tournament play. He begged me to let him back in, choking up in tears by the end. Even though he was one of my biggest spenders, I simply could not tolerate a man in his forties cheating against children in my store. I even put up a "No Big Dave" sign. The kids loved it.

I later learned that Big Dave was banned from many of the tournaments and stores in the area. Being a computer guy, he turned to selling his cards on the internet, long before it was a common practice. Online, it doesn't matter how obnoxious or smelly you are, as long as you have the lowest price.

Chapter 14

My first couple of months of store ownership went better than I expected, and it just kept growing from there. The store hours were 11:00 AM to 7:00 PM. *Magic* remained the best seller, but I also developed a small group of card and comic collectors who became regulars because of the discounted prices I offered.

I had plenty of access to merchandise, between several distributors and all the shows and markets I went to. Also, as word about my store spread, people started bringing their collectibles to sell to me. The more money the store made, the more inventory I added.

Business was slow during the early hours, and I used that time to put together card sets, bag and board comics, and prepare for shows. The store always got busier on weekdays after school let out. Even the slowest days had a busy period. Kids came in to play and trade *Magic* cards, spending any spare cash on packs or singles.

As with the flea markets and shows, there was always a risk of shoplifters. I never had a security camera. Even if I did, they aren't that effective in dealing with small thefts like I faced. Kids loved to try to fit a pack or two in their pocket, and having a tape of it after the fact didn't do any good. Instead I enforced my own brand of justice.

I put up a sign that said: "SHOPLIFTERS WILL BE PERSECUTED". People often asked, "Isn't that supposed to say prosecuted?" My answer was "No." Most of the potential shoplifters were young kids, so calling the cops wasn't an option, and scaring them off wasn't too hard.

I was direct with kids who looked suspicious to me, saying as soon as they walked in, "Hi, how are you? Don't even think about stealing!" When I caught a shoplifter trying to steal any merchandise, I took the items back and banned them for life.

I ran my store like a big flea market setup, or, as my friend Steve called it, a hegdesh. Steve had a store much like mine in Scotch Plains, New Jersey. Although we sold similar merchandise, his store was equipped with state-of-the-art wall slats, jewelry store show cases, and professional lighting. My store, on the other hand, had cheap lamps, wire racks for comics, and portable 3' x 1' cases on folding tables.

Despite the apparent class difference, we got along well and did business together for several years. After the store had been going for a year, we merged our comic orders to get a bigger discount. He would also sell boxes of *Magic* cards to me at wholesale. Steve always ordered more than he needed, knowing I'd buy anything extra. Since I did shows and flea markets along with the store, I sold way more *Magic* than he did. I knew when I ran low I could always call him up for a few more boxes.

Steve also owned a bar, and we usually met there because it was closer to my home than his store. One Wednesday in June of 1995, I met him there to get more boxes of *Ice Age*, the newest *Magic* set. I bought six boxes of boosters and two boxes of starter decks from him. Wednesday was karaoke night at Steve's bar, and after we finished our deal, he began trying to get me to go up on stage.

Steve was a terrible singer but he was really into karaoke. Since he was the owner of the bar, everyone cheered him on and he gave out many free drinks. He insisted that I give it a try. I had never tried it before and didn't like the song list there, but he persisted. He finally offered me a free booster box of *Ice Age* if I got on stage!

Since those boxes were going for $90 at the time, I did not flinch at that offer. I chose to sing "Time is on My Side" by the Rolling Stones. I thought it was a decent performance, though I was probably no better than Steve. I actually grew to like karaoke. To this day, the Rolling Stones are always my band of choice for karaoke.

While my singing skills are not entirely relevant to my story here, the *Ice Age* expansion certainly is. The set was something of a savior for *Magic*, which had hit a rough patch after a prosperous first year. After the success of *Arabian Nights*, Wizards of the Coast continued releasing new themed expansion sets every few months. The first few were popular, but when *Fallen Empires* came out in 1994, that all changed. By the time it arrived, news about *Magic* had spread, and the orders were massive. Wizards of the Coast printed so much that it tanked, and packs ended up selling for just a dollar each.

Part of the problem with *Fallen Empires* was that it just wasn't very good. Wizards of the Coast had been designing progressively weaker cards, to avoid outclassing earlier releases. This meant there were not many desirable or expensive cards in *Fallen Empires*.

The company learned their lesson with their next expansion. *Ice Age* upped the power level and introduced some new things to the game. It was the first standalone expansion, so newcomers no longer had to go back and collect the older base sets before they could start playing. *Ice Age* contained mostly new cards with a unified story and aesthetic. But it also included basic land cards and reintroduced starter decks with revised, up-to-date rules. This made *Ice Age* a great starting point for new players, while still holding enough high-profile cards for the seasoned player.

Ice Age also brought a new twist on the land cards. The basic mountains, forests, plains, islands, and swamps had remained unchanged for the first couple of years. *Ice Age* introduced snow-covered lands, which were snowy versions of the original five land types. Certain cards interacted differently with snow-covered lands. Some creatures became more powerful when you had more of the lands, and there were spells that couldn't be used unless you had a snow-covered land in play.

These new land versions drew a lot of attention when they debuted, and people thought they would have a permanent impact on the game.

As it turned out, they did not, and are now little more than a footnote in the history of *Magic*. But people were snapping them up for a while, thinking they were going to skyrocket in value. One such investor was Leo, who is probably the customer with the worst business sense I have ever met.

Leo had been a customer of my store for close to a year when *Ice Age* was released. He regularly dropped hundreds of dollars, and he turned into a gold mine when the snow-covered lands came out. He'd take all I could find for 50 cents apiece. The true value of the cards, even back then, was only a few cents. But Leo thought they were going to rise to five bucks or more in the future and by then he'd have thousands of snow-covered lands.

When Wizards of the Coast introduced premium holographic cards a few years later, Leo was even worse. Starting with *Urza's Legacy*, it was possible to find a shiny, holographic version of every card in the set. This practice continues to this day and it does raise the value of the card. But only the cards that are already scarce, and thus expensive, see any significant increase in price. With those, the holographic version can be worth up the three times the price of the normal version.

Leo bought every single holo I could muster up. He took the commons for 25¢, uncommons for 50¢, and rares for $2 and up. I was able to buy these cards from other customers who did not care about them. I had another pile for him every time he came in, and he told me to keep them coming. I had customers scooping up as many holos as they could when they went to various tournaments. They sold them to me and I sold them to Leo. Leo kept taking them even when I had hundreds at a time.

Leo liked to play in the *Magic* tournaments as well. He was sixty years old when I first met him, and like most older players, he played slowly and badly. Most of his games were disqualified for taking too long. But beyond his bad play and terrible investments, the most defining characteristic of Leo was his smell.

Leo reeked. That is an understatement. I mean, Leo smelled really, truly, and utterly awful. It was the moldy, musty stink of death. I didn't want to turn him away since he was my best customer in terms of dollars spent. But his scent was unbearable, and something had to be done.

So when Leo came in, I started sneaking behind him to spray him with Lysol. I'd also spray down the counters nearby, to avoid suspicion. I don't think he ever caught on. But either way, every time he came in I hit him with the Lysol.

One day, Leo brought me a box of old comics that he wanted to sell. The store was very busy, so he left them for me to look at later. I didn't have a chance to look until after the store closed. When I opened the box, I was shocked to see books like *X-Men* #1 and *Batman* and *Superman* comics from the 30s and 40s. In mint condition, Leo's collection would be worth millions.

Unfortunately, I realized immediately that they were not in mint condition. They were in the same condition as Leo: horrid. They were also infested with silverfish. I was disgusted that he had brought this potential infestation into my store, and immediately took the box and put it on the porch.

I called Leo and told him where his box of comics was and that he needed to get it out of here. It was snowing that night, and by the time Leo picked them up the next morning they were totally soaked, ruining them further, if that was possible.

Leo was pretty pissed off, but I told him about a comic book show coming up where he might be able to get rid of them. He managed to sell them to some crazy comic lady for $150. Even though they were in deplorable condition, if she cleaned them up a bit she probably was able to make a decent profit, because some of the most expensive books of all time were in that tattered box.

I could handle Leo, but a box full of silverfish was just too much. He came to the store less often after that, and once he discovered the internet he stopped coming entirely. Even though he spent a considerable amount of money, I didn't really miss him. A can of Lysol lasted much longer after that.

Chapter 15

While I was a bit apprehensive about opening a store, the first few years went better than expected. As it turned out, I had had good timing.

Similar shops were popping up every day. Within a few years, almost every town in New Jersey had a collectibles shop, usually a sports card store. Some towns had multiple outlets selling collectibles.

I saw a statistic that in 1995 there were over 5000 baseball card shops in the USA. That did not include comic book stores or kiosks in the malls. In addition, stores like Walmart began selling many of the same products, starting with sports cards but soon expanding to all kinds of collectibles.

I remember the first time I saw Toys "R" Us selling *Magic* cards. Kids were sitting in the aisles ripping open boxes of packs, taking the cards they wanted, and leaving the rest lying on the floor. It was several years before they started producing blister packs, which are much harder to open.

Despite growing competition, all these products were so hot that there was still plenty of money to be made. To stay ahead of the competition, you had to stay ahead of the curve. You had to be the first to jump when a hot product came out, because you never knew how long it would stay hot.

One item that had a brief moment in the spotlight was Tickle Me Elmo. Released in late 1996, Elmo was *the* hot gift that Christmas. The talking doll from Sesame Street had everyone going crazy. The retail price was $28.99, but when I was lucky enough to get my hands on some, I could sell them for $100 each. Some people were trying to get up to $200. *The Daily News* reported one being sold for $1500, which only increased the fervor of the Elmo shoppers.

One day, a few weeks before Christmas, I noticed a Tickle Me Elmo display in a Toys "R" Us. There was a sign that said two per customer. I muscled my way through the crowd surrounding the display, and quickly wheeled away with two in my cart. As I made my way through the store, a woman approached me and offered $100 for the pair. Since I hadn't even bought them yet, this was the easiest sale I ever made!

While cash was flowing in from every angle, it was hard to manage everything. Between flea markets and shows, constantly needing to pick up more merchandise, and now scouring toy stores regularly, I barely had any time to be in my store. Though I have always preferred to do everything myself as much as possible, I was then forced to hire an employee.

The individual I first picked to work in my store had lived in Hackettstown all his life. I first met him at a collectibles show in the Hackettstown Mall a few years before I opened the store. For as long as I have known him, he has worn black gym shorts all year round, usually paired with a torn and dirty t-shirt. His name was Blam.

Blam never had much money to spend but often hung out at my table at shows, talking trash with anyone who would listen. Once he found my store, he did the same thing there. He claimed to be a big *Dungeons & Dragons* player from way back in the day. He was terrible at *Magic* so he didn't play it, claiming he didn't like it. But he found his true calling when he discovered *Warhammer*.

Warhammer is an intricate game that uses metal or plastic figurines that players have to assemble and paint by hand. There is a detailed storyline behind it, with a fantasy setting involving orcs and elves. Perhaps even more popular was *Warhammer 40,000,* more commonly known as *Warhammer 40K.* This version had a science fiction setting, with space marines fighting aliens. The figures were quite expensive, and some of the vehicles cost hundreds of dollars.

My store carried the rule books for both versions of the game, a good selection of figures and a few vehicles, as well as all the necessary paint, knives, and glue. While this game did not explode into mainstream popularity like many things in the 90s, it did become a very popular hobby for a dedicated group of players. I started reserving my game tables on Sundays for *Warhammer.* There was a tournament twice a month, one for *Warhammer* and one for *Warhammer 40K.* It was always a colorful scene, with some players toting huge armies of beautifully detailed pieces.

Once I started carrying *Warhammer* in my store, Blam became a regular. Surprisingly, he was pretty good at painting the figures. As with *Magic,* he was not very good at the game, and 12- and 13-year-old kids could beat him handily. But he loved

Warhammer and was in my store every day, playing, painting, and bullshitting.

When the time came to hire someone a couple of days a week, I figured he spent so much time in the store, why not put him to work? He was 27, didn't have a job, and still lived with his parents, so he was more than agreeable to $5 an hour. In addition, I sold him anything in the store for what I had paid for it. I agreed to special order anything he wanted, and sell that to him at cost as well. He was also allowed to paint his figures on a table in the back when there was no one in the store. Overall, it was a great deal for him.

I put him in the store for the slowest parts of the day at first, scheduling his shift before the kids got out of school. He would come in on time, which was nice, but he always brought a huge bag full of McDonald's food with him which would stink up the place. This turned out to be part of a bigger problem; Blam was a slob, and the more I told him he needed to dress and act nicer, the worse he got.

Customers began complaining about his appearance and the smell of the store. Blam got very defensive when I tried talking to him about his hygiene. When I asked him to consider eating before or after his three-hour shift, he claimed that he did many good things for the store and that I took him for granted. Then he threatened to tell his friends to stop coming in if I continued to bother him.

Blam was fired on the spot. His friends kept coming back, but not him. Soon after Blam's departure, I hired a college kid named Bill. He was a hard worker and I paid him well. I also gave him merchandise at cost, which was what he valued most. Bill was a great employee and worked for me for many years, the exact opposite of Blam. I had many other good employees over the years at my store and the flea markets, including my son James.

Chapter 16

The decade was half over, but the best item of the 90s was still to come. In the summer of 1996

I first encountered it in a show at the South Brunswick firehouse. It was a Saturday and I was rained out of the flea market I had planned to do. My buddy Jeff had two tables at the show and said he could sell me one. He sold strictly sports cards, so we agreed that I would only put out *Magic* and comics.

Before the show started, we each took a turn watching the tables so the other could walk around the room and scan for deals. It was a pretty slow day, and nothing caught my eye -- until I saw a guy who was selling nothing but Beanie Babies. I had heard something about them before, but this was my first time seeing them in person. His table, piled high with the colorful stuffed animals, stood out amongst the sports card setups.

As soon as I saw them, something hit me: these were going to be the next big thing. I don't know why but I just felt it, so I decided to keep an eye on the Beanie table throughout the show. He did not sell many that day, but I did notice something intriguing. These shows always brought in a fair number of women who tagged along with husbands or boyfriends. They did not typically spend any money – but the women that day were buying Beanies. The kids who were at the show all seemed interested in them as well.

The seller's Beanies were marked from $6 to $10. I don't know what he was basing his prices on, as this was well before Beanie price guides started coming out. Towards the end of the show, I decided to see if he would sell me the whole lot of them. I always brought a wad of cash with me to every show in case I ran across a deal like this one. He had 207 Beanies with him. I offered him $1000 for everything and he took it.

When I brought the Beanies back to the table, Jeff thought I was playing a trick on him and started laughing uncontrollably. He didn't believe that I had actually bought them. He laughed even harder when I said how much I had paid. I must admit, I felt a little nervous at this point. I was even more nervous when I realized that they retailed for just over what I paid for them. Had I thrown away a thousand bucks?

All I could do was put them out and see how they sold. I left a nice variety behind at the store and attended the flea market in Marshalls Creek, Pennsylvania, the next day. For the store, I put a shelf of Beanies next to the register at $8 each. The rest went with me to Marshall's Creek, where I put them out at the same price. That Sunday, I sold six in the store and fifteen at the flea market. I was pretty happy about that, so I changed the sign in front of my store to say simply, "Beanie Babies." That's all I had to say and new customers were arriving daily.

Next, I needed to know where to get my hands on some more Beanies – and quickly. I started with some research to find out what Beanie Babies really were. As it turned out, they had been around longer than I thought. Beanies were, and still are, made by Ty Inc, a company that has been making plush toys since the 80s. Beanie Babies looked very similar to a regular plush toy. The big difference was that these had considerably less stuffing, instead using a mix of traditional cotton stuffing and plastic pellets.

The design of Beanies allowed them to be put in creative poses more easily than any other plush toy on the market. In addition, each individual Beanie had a name and a birthdate printed inside a heart-shaped tag hanging from it. The first wave of Beanie Babies came out in 1994, and consisted of Legs the Frog, Squealer the Pig, Spot the Dog, Flash the Dolphin, Splash the Whale, Chocolate the Moose, Patti the Platypus, Brownie the Bear, and Pinchers the Lobster.

By the time I stumbled onto Beanies, those were already out of production and rapidly rising in price. Ty, which had once been a humble plush manufacturer, was keen to squeeze the most cash they could out of their surprise hit. They had an intricate schedule, with new Beanies coming out all the time. To balance this, they had a practice they called 'retiring' a Beanie, where they stopped making any more of that particular model. Once retired, an average Beanie's value on the secondary market would jump up from $5 to between $8 and $15, which is where they would start out during the first week or two of release. Teddy bear Beanie Babies were the most popular, and started out even higher at $15 to $30. Most of the first wave Beanies took a few years to be retired, but only the ones with the original edition hangtag fetched a notable sum.

In the first few years, Beanies were only sold to gift shops, the kinds of stores that sold flowers and greeting cards. I really wanted to get a direct account with Ty, and even attended Toy Fair, the annual toy retailer's convention in New York City, in my campaign to get one. By then Beanie Babies were taking hold of America as a national phenomenon. Ty told me they were not taking any new accounts at the time.

Still determined to get an account, I sent Ty a check for $1000. A week later, I saw that the check had been cashed. After hearing nothing from them for another week, I called the number for the Ty representative in my area, which I had gotten at Toy Fair. I let him know that I had $1000 on account and was ready to order. He told me that he knew nothing about it and could not take an order from me. I never did get a Ty account, and they played dumb about my $1000 deposit until I paid a lawyer a hundred bucks for a threatening letter.

If I had been able to get a Ty account, I could be a rich man today. But I didn't, so I had to spend thousands of dollars buying the hot Beanies from secondary sources, when it would have only cost me hundreds at wholesale. It didn't matter, though, because Beaniemania was real. And I always found a way to get more Beanies.

I immediately put up a "Buying Beanies" sign in my store, and it stayed up for several years. That did not yield nearly enough stock so I had to find other connections. I met my first connection, Mr. Cho, right at the Marshall's Creek flea market where I went most weekends. Mr. Cho owned seven gift stores but never put any Beanies out for sale in his stores.

Mr. Cho would sell me the common, less desirable Beanies for $4. While every Beanie under the sun was in high demand at that point, only the bears, new releases, and Holiday Beanies were really valuable. In a really good week, I could sell as many as a thousand of the common Beanies for $5 each, as long as Mr. Cho could keep them coming.

One day I heard an advertisement for a doll show on the radio, and I thought that might be a gold mine for Beanies. The show ran over a Friday and Saturday, so I was able to go on Friday and not miss any flea market days. It was a huge show with over 200 dealers. Surprisingly, however, there were very few Beanies.

After a bit of searching, I found one lady who had all the new releases. She was selling them for $6. I talked to her for a while, then told her I wanted to buy quantity. She said I could take as many as I wanted for $4 each. I immediately agreed. That weekend I sold every one, at $8 apiece. Beanie Babies always seemed to sell for the highest price on the secondary market when they first came out.

For the next few years, I met that lady at the Wendy's in Flemington, New Jersey, every Friday at 8 PM. She had dozens of bags full of all kinds of Beanies, all unopened. I always paid her a fair price. For example, I might get a dozen of Radar the Bat for $30 apiece and sell them for $50 each. She was thrilled, since she had nowhere else to sell them above retail except the occasional doll show. She sold Beanies in her doll store for $6 each and always let me buy the common ones for $4, and I paid $8 for the teddy bears. When something hot came out, as when Ty released Gobbles the Turkey for Thanksgiving, we would negotiate a price that worked for both of us.

For Thanksgiving weekend when Gobbles came out, I bought a dozen from her at $33 each. I put them out at $45 and they sold very quickly. When I was down to my last one, two ladies started pushing each other, vying for the plush. They almost got into a fist fight, trying to spend $45 on a stuffed animal that retails for $5!

At that point I realized two things. First, Beanies were not going anywhere, at least not anytime soon. And second, I had to raise the price when I got more Gobbles.

Gobbles was not even that notable a Beanie. There were some, like him, that had their moments of popularity, but every so often Ty would release a special Beanie that would immediately shoot up to over $100. And of those, none created more of a frenzy than Princess.

Princess, a purple bear with a white embroidered rose on her chest, was made in memory Princess Diana after she passed away in 1997. This was probably the most anticipated Beanie of all time.

By this time, there were collectibles shows just for Beanie Babies, and I was doing one the weekend Princess was released. I *needed* Princess for that show – at that moment, she was the only Beanie that mattered.

The Flemington Wendy's lady was able to get me three dozen of the purple bears. She didn't put any out in her store, instead selling them all to me. Although they only cost her $2.75 each, she wanted $160 for each one, firm. I really did not want to pay that much, but since I had a Beanie show to do, I bit the bullet and took them all.

The show was in the Ledgewood mall in New Jersey. There were only four other dealers who had Princess. Before the show started, they all colluded and agreed to sell them for $250 each. Realistically, this meant they would let them go for $225, maybe $200 at the lowest. I put mine out for $190.

As they saw me selling many of them, the group of dealers complained to the show promoter that I was selling Princess too cheaply. When he came to me to tell me about the complaint, I simply told him that I am asking $190 for a bear with a suggested retail price of $5. He offered no further argument. I sold all three dozen that weekend.

By the next weekend, Princess was $125. The weekend after that, $100. Ty inevitably put out more waves of the bear, flooding the market. Everyone who wanted a Princess got at least one. The bear, once royalty, ended up on the $5 table with the rest of the peasants.

Another Beanie that made a splash was Maple, a bear originally only available in Canada. Someone I knew drove over 300 miles up to Canada and brought some back. I paid $100 each and sold them for $150. My price was actually low, as the average was around $200. The demand for these became so high, and so many people were traveling to Canada to get Maple, that cars were getting searched at the border.

I always had to pay a premium to get the newest Beanies as they were released. For example, if a new bear came out and I had to pay $10 each, I would charge $15 each. Customers asked me why the price was so high, and my reply was that I had to sell them for more because I had to pay more to get them upon release. I also told them that if they were willing to wait, they'd probably be on the $5 table in a few weeks. Most of the customers still bought it at the higher price. And the Beanies usually ended up on the $5 table.

One day, I noticed that the teller in my bank had a Humphrey the Camel on the counter at her window. Humphrey was an old Beanie, one of the first to be retired. A mint condition one with the tag would fetch about $1200 at that time. Hers didn't have a tag and wasn't in great condition. I told her the story and offered her $300 on the spot for it. She said she needed to think about it. I was going to a Beanie show that weekend, so I told her she had until Friday. When Friday came around, she came to the store and asked me for $700. When I told her $300 was my best offer, she left.

Coincidentally, I bought a tagless Humphrey at the Beanie show that weekend for $200 and sold it for $300. The lady from the bank ultimately came back to my store about two years later, ready to take the $300. I told her that I was only willing to pay $50 at that time. She declined and left my store again in a huff.

The value of a Beanie totally depended on the condition of the tag. The bank teller probably took off the tag as soon as she got her Humphrey, not realizing that it would be worth anything. There were plenty of people who had bought Beanies for their kids before they became popular, and then wanted to cash in. But unless it was one of the most expensive and rare Beanies, it had to have the tag in mint condition.

Of course, that just opened another avenue for profit. Specially designed tag protectors came out, and people bought them by the fistfuls. They were just a simple sleeve of plastic that slipped over the tag. They came twenty to a package, in a plastic fishbowl with fifty packages in it.

Having gotten the tag protectors as soon as they appeared, I was going through five fishbowls a week between the store and the flea market until all the other dealers started selling them. Next came clamshell tag protectors that snapped closed over the tag. Soon everyone was replacing their tag sleeves with the clamshells. Again, I was selling hundreds of these weekly.

The protectors kept the tag in perfect shape, but a mint Beanie also needed protection from wear and even dust. Mark, a friend with a store in Brooklyn, came up with an idea for a Beanie case. He went to Bronx Plastics with a design for a simple plastic box that could hold one Beanie. Mark, another dealer, and myself all pooled our money and had thousands of these cases made.

We rented a box truck and split the first order three ways. The cases cost us $1 each. I put them in my store at $4 each and they sold like crazy. My tiny store went through about 200 that first week.

The next weekend, I paid an unemployed customer of mine to bring as many cases as he could to the Marshall's Creek flea market. He showed up around 10 AM on Saturday with hundreds of cases wedged into his big old Cadillac. Once he pulled up to my spot, his job was to just sell Beanie cases while I handled everything else. We sold all that he brought at $4 apiece, then sold out another full load the next day.

We repeated the success of that first weekend for several more weeks. We were probably not the first to manufacture Beanie cases, and we were definitely not the last. My monopoly on them soon ended as all the other dealers found their own sources for Beanie cases. I got a bigger truck so I could travel to flea markets with about a hundred cases along with the rest of my merchandise. I lowered the price to $3 each or three for $8, and was still able to sell close to a hundred every weekend for several months.

Mark also designed an improved clamshell tag protector. He sold me cases of a thousand for $30. I sold them loose, three for 25¢. I was able to churn out thousands. I offered a wholesale price for buyers who purchased at least 100. Between tag protectors and the cases, selling Beanie supplies became almost a full-time job in itself.

Less than a year after I had first seen a Beanie Baby, it seemed like they had pervaded every aspect of my life. In one Atlantic City casino, I saw a row of slot machine that gave out Beanies as well as cash prizes. They were all just common Beanies, but there was a line for those slot machines every time I walked by, day or night.

One day, a car salesman showed up at my store from the Ford dealership where I had bought my truck. He bought twenty Beanies from me that day, and a few days later he bought twenty more. They were giving away a free Beanie with every test drive. The dealership ran the promotion for three months, during which they bought almost 500 Beanies.

Since it seemed like everybody in the world wanted Beanies, I often used them as a commodity. I almost never bought lunch or breakfast -- I traded a Beanie for a meal. People were always coming into my store or up to me at the market trying to trade for Beanies. And I paid in Beanies for at least half the merchandise I picked up at shows.

At one point the reach of Beanies was so intense that it even crossed paths with my old life. Jerry Garcia, always the heart of the Grateful Dead, passed away in 1995. Had I still been in the business of making tie-dyes, I might have been out of a job at that point. The Grateful Dead broke up and all the hippies went back to, well, wherever they could go. But to commemorate Jerry's passing, Ty made a special rainbow tie-dyed bear called Garcia.

While Garcia was a very popular Beanie when it came out, the price really spiked when he was retired in 1997. Ty introduced a new version of the bear with a peace sign on the chest named, appropriately, Peace. This new bear was also highly desirable but never reached the value that Garcia did. The price of Garcia shot up from $20 to $75.

Someone I knew had been hoarding Garcia beanies for a while and brought me a dozen a week for almost twenty weeks. He charged me $33 a bear and I sold out at $50 apiece every week. While I had of course been sad to hear about Jerry's passing, it was nice to still be making a living from his legacy, years after the fact.

The peak of Beanie Babies' invasion of mass culture came when Ty teamed up with McDonald's. The collision of these two billion-dollar companies resulted in the Teenie Beanies. These were miniature versions of popular Beanies that were included in Happy Meals for kids. They became an instant frenzy, and McDonald's stores were selling out of them overnight.

Ten different Teenie Beanies came out in the first series in 1997 and they were only available for a short promotional period. In New Jersey, Teenie Beanies cost me $2.12 each, including the sales tax. With that first wave, I was able to sell them for $5 each at flea markets. I would go to the drive-thru and order a hundred at a time. But while I purchased over 5000 Happy Meals, I never once took the food. I would simply drive up to the drive-thru window, order 100 happy meals, and tell them to hold the food.

A year later, series two of the Teenie Beanies was released, this one including twelve different critters. This was at the peak of Beaniemania. Ty and McDonald's were much more prepared this time, but even with greatly increased production, nothing could satisfy the unimaginable demand. The second series of Teenie Beanies caused numerous fights, injuries, and arrests at various McDonald's locations.

While McDonald's was running out of Teenie Beanies long before the promotion was supposed to end, it seemed like every vendor at every show, market, and event of any kind had a few Teenie Beanies out for sale. Many dealers were trying to sell the full set of twelve. I was so busy that I decided to not even bother with series two. There were long lines at McDonald's, with strict rules on how many you could get, unlike the previous year when I got hundreds at a time.

I tried to steer clear of this wave of Teenie Beanie madness until a local McDonald's manager came directly to my store and offered them to me by the case. I paid $1 each and sold them for $2, selling over a thousand Teenie Beanies this way. You couldn't beat the price; I was cheaper than McDonald's.

The third and final wave of 90s Teenie Beanies appeared in 1999. McDonald's, again, drew huge crowds to collect all twelve Teenie Babies from wave three. But I avoided them almost entirely because the secondary market had become flooded. Beaniemania peaked with series two in 1998. After that, what had risen so rapidly was bound to fall.

Chapter 17

Everyone involved with Beanie Babies was having a grand old time in 1998. Collectors filled their attics with treasures they valued more than gold. People quit their jobs to become full-time Beanie dealers. Everyone said that Beanies were so popular and so big that they could only keep going up.

In the fall of 1998 the Unofficial Beanie Baby Handbook was released. This was the first dedicated price guide for Beanies. While the prices were not very accurate, it was an instant success. The book had a $10 cover price, and I purchased a thousand at $4.50 each. That Thanksgiving weekend I sold about 800 copies of the handbook at Marshall's Creek. It was a cold weekend, a holiday, and the market was only moderately busy. Most people out there were looking for Beanies, and the handbooks flew at $8. By the end of the day, it seemed like every person in the crowd was carrying an Unofficial Beanie Baby Handbook.

Ultimately that book serves as a testament to everything that was wrong with Beaniemania. They were supposed to be innocent children's toys, but Beanies turned into a monster that brought out the greed in everyone. The Beanie Baby handbook included projections for what the Beanies would be worth in ten years. Every Beanie was scheduled to rise in price, most astronomically. Not one was predicted to decline in value

Everyone thought they had gold. As it turns out, Beanies that were predicted to be worth thousands of dollars in ten years were selling for just a dollar or two by 2008. And the vast majority of people held onto their Beanies until it was too late. I'm sure there are plenty of collectors who bought them out of love for the product, and who still have and cherish their Beanies today. But most just cared about the money

Though it seems downright silly today, there were a couple of years where Beanies were an actual status symbol. No one believed in this concept more than the owner of the jewelry store across the street from my store. At the peak of the Beanie craze he decided to start selling high-priced Beanie Babies. Next to a display of Beanies he was trying to sell, he had a huge curio cabinet filled with his "personal collection," complete with a sign saying they were not for sale.

He would come to my store and try to buy my high-end Beanies, offering insultingly low prices. He was relentless about it, and eventually I had to ban him from my store. To make it worse, he put ridiculously high prices on the Beanies in his store. For example, while I was selling Tabasco the Bull for $70, he wanted $199.99 for his, right across the street!

He even had the rarest Beanie of all in his store. The royal blue Peanut the Elephant was, and surely still is, the most desirable Beanie Baby in the world. It became so valuable because the color was changed to a lighter blue, making the royal blue version short printed and extremely rare. There were reports of it going as high as $5000. The guy from the jewelry store wanted $6,999 for his.

A couple of years after that guy started selling Beanie Babies, his store went completely out of business. It was a family business that had been in town for over forty years. I am sure that if he had never gotten involved with Beanies, his store might still be in business today. Why would a jewelry store ever sell stuffed animals? Because they were Beanie Babies, and they were everywhere.

While there were a few older rare Beanies like Peanut that could fetch thousands of dollars, I never dealt too much in these. During the craze, it was much easier to sell in huge quantity than worry about having the rarest Beanies. But that is not to say I didn't sell my fair share of high-ticket Beanies.

Caw the Crow was the most expensive Beanie I ever sold myself. It was one of the first Beanies retired, and a good customer requested it. Caw was quite scarce and the customer told me she was willing to pay up to $1000 for a mint one. I found one for $750 and sold it to her for $900.

The most expensive Beanie I ever saw sold was a wingless Quackers the Duck. The first wave of this Beanie was produced without wings, which were added after people realized how silly it looked without them. Since there were not a lot of wingless ones they were worth big cash. The lady next to me at a monthly Beanie show sold one for $2500.

The next month, at the same show, she had another wingless Quackers in her display. She told me that she had bought another one from the same source. She paid $1800 each. She did not sell the second wingless Quackers that night. I did not see her again until years later, after the Beanie crash. She still had the second wingless Quackers.

Everyone wanted a piece of the Beanie Baby cash grab, and for a while it worked. In 1998 Ty partnered with the New York Yankees for a Beanie giveaway. On May 17th, they gave a Valentino to everyone who came to the game. Valentino was already on the market, going for up to $15. I decided to go to the game to get a few of them.

I brought a stack of cash with me to see if I could pick some up cheaply. I got my Beanie at the door when I entered the stadium. I noticed that, while this Valentino was no different from any other Valentino, it came with a card that said it was a special limited-edition Beanie from this game. I realized that all I needed was the card and not the actual Beanie, which I could find easily.

I took a walk around the lobby of Yankee Stadium offering people $20 for just the card. Since they could keep the Beanie, some were convinced. By the third inning I had about thirty of these cards. Yankees pitcher David Wells was throwing a no-hitter, so it became harder to get the cards as the game went on. I started offering $30, and by the end of the game I had a total of 53 cards, including my own.

David Wells not only pitched a no-hitter, it was a perfect game. This made the cards soar in value. The next Tuesday, at the show I did every week in Parsippany, dealers were selling Valentino with the card in a case for between $250 to $300. I bought a dozen regular Valentinos for $8 each, and matched them with a case and commemorative card. They sold out for $200 each. After that first dozen, I sold two more of these combos in my store and ten at flea markets. I sold the rest of the cards to other dealers at $150 a card. Within two weeks the cards were completely sold out.

Shortly after this, another sports Beanie became popular. These were not actually produced by Ty, but one of the countless knockoff products. They were baseball bears made locally in New Jersey. Each bear had the name and number of a player on its back. I thought they were very poorly made but they sold great for a few months.

I didn't deal too heavily with these sports bears, but a few were great sellers. The most popular were the Sammy Sosa and Mark McGwire bears. The real-life players were involved in a race to break the single-season home run record that year, which created a frenzy for anything with their names on them. Most regular players went for $5 to $10 but I could get $50 for a pair of Sosa and McGwire.

After the success of the baseball bears, similar products came out for every sport. None of these other bears caught on. This was 1998, right at the peak of the height of Beaniemania. Beanies were still hot, but a glut of related products started hitting the market. Things like the Beanie Baby trading cards met with mixed success.

One of the last standout Beanies from the peak was Clubby. This bear came in a small lunchbox-sized zipper case with a commemorative coin, stickers, and more. It was exclusively available to members of the official Beanie Baby club. I signed up at the mall to get one. They were selling for $100 when they first came out. A week later they dropped to $50, and then to $25. Ty produced a Clubby bear every year after that, but they were only valuable for the first couple weeks.

Ty ultimately produced Beanies for every theme or event you could imagine. There were Beanies for every holiday, and licensed Beanies for every sport or pop culture trend. These special releases always went for a higher price than other Beanies. But the more that came out, the less it mattered. Ty also introduced several other lines of products, like the larger-sized Beanie Buddies, but none of them made a huge impact.

By the year 2000, even retiring a Beanie didn't matter anymore. They were producing so many that there were more than enough for anyone who wanted them. More and more people came into the store to sell their entire collections, and eventually I had to take down my "Buying Beanies" sign.

Customers who had been buying Beanies from me for years were coming to cash in and leaving utterly defeated. I alienated a large portion of my customer base just by offering them what their Beanies were worth. But before this, while Beanies were still hovering around their peak, other crazes were hitting the public, including one that would outlive Beaniemania: Pokémon.

Chapter 18

Of all the wild crazes of the 90s, the one with the most staying power is surely *Pokémon*. This huge franchise permeated every aspect of pop culture, and is still loved by fans of all ages today. It grew far beyond its origin as a Japanese video game in 1996. The spirit of the 90s is truly embodied in *Pokémon*'s simple slogan: "Gotta catch 'em all!"

Pokémon are creatures that each have unique abilities, strengths, and weaknesses. Most resemble real animals, and fall into different categories – fire, ice, psychic, and more. Your mission in playing the game is to catch the various Pokémon by pitting your critters against other Pokémon masters. Beginning with the easiest to capture, you work your way to the Elite Four, taking your place among the greatest Pokémon trainers of all time once you have caught them all. There were 151 Pokémon in the original generation, though hundreds more have come along since then.

This basic premise spun off multiple variations in Japan, including a popular cartoon, a trading card game, and endless waves of Pokémon-themed merchandise. By the time *Pokémon* arrived in the United States in 1998, everything was in place to make it the biggest media franchise of the 90s and beyond. The video game, the cartoon, and most importantly to this story, the trading card game, all hit America within a few months of each other. Each one just intensified *Pokémon*'s grip on the end of the 90s.

Beaniemania was still raging when the *Pokémon* cartoon began airing on American TV stations. But *Pokémon* really took off with the release of the video game a few weeks later. There were two versions of the game, *Red* and *Blue*, each with exclusive Pokémon not found on the other version. The only way to have them all was to trade between the two versions. It was an ingenious marketing ploy: not only did every kid beg for *Pokémon*, many got their parents to buy essentially the same game twice!

Pokémon Red and *Blue* were played on the Nintendo Gameboy, a portable video game system. Big stores like Walmart and Toys "R" Us repeatedly sold out of both *Pokémon* versions as well as the Gameboy itself. I avoided competing with the big box stores at first, but eventually the games proved so popular that I started selling Gameboys, *Pokémon*, and a few other video games. But all that came after the stuffed Pikachus.

Pikachu, a bright yellow, electric mouse Pokémon, was a main character in the cartoon and the mascot for the *Pokémon* universe. My 12-inch Pikachus were not even officially licensed products, just cheap bootlegs. I came across them one day at the Marshall's Creek flea market, when I noticed an Asian guy with a setup on the front row.

Since this was unusual for someone who was not an established vendor, I naturally had to investigate. To my surprise his booth was filled with those stuffed Pikachus and he was only asking $5 each! I bought 50, and between the store and shows during the week, I sold them all by the next weekend.

Pokémon was just starting to catch on, so those bootleg Pikachus were the only item I could get at first. Japanese products soon began filling the void until Hasbro started making merchandise for the American fans. There were *Pokémon* stickers, figures, trading cards, and plenty more – and they all sold. The first big item produced for the U.S. market was a line of PVC Pokémon figures that came in Pokéballs. They were carried in all kinds of stores, and the first wave sold out everywhere.

While the video game, the show, and the first few products were all instant successes, the *Pokémon* trading card game took the mania to a new level. For the first time, kids could actually collect them all. And for a while it did seem like every kid in America was collecting *Pokémon* cards. Most didn't even play the game, but every kid had to have them.

Released in January 1999, *Pokémon* trading cards dominated that last year of the decade, and had become the most popular item in my store by the turn of the century. It was nice for me as a retailer – you can only sell someone one or two copies of the video game, but with new *Pokémon* sets coming out every few months, kids returned week after week for more cards. The only limit was how much their parents were willing to spend.

The card game began in Japan, and was based on *Magic: The Gathering*, using many of the same rules. In fact, the company that had created *Magic*, Wizards of the Coast, also distributed the translated *Pokémon* game in the United States. The first wave of *Pokémon* cards in English included small first-edition logos. With a frenzy already well underway, prices for these original *Pokémon* cards skyrocketed.

Wizards of the Coast had strict limits on dealer quantities of the first edition. I got the maximum – one case, containing six boxes of card packs. I only got that much because I already had an account with Wizards of the Coast and ordered large quantities of *Magic*. I didn't inflate my price and was completely sold out in under a week. For me, this confirmed that *Pokémon* was going to be huge.

The next day I drove around the New York metropolitan area, buying up all the first-edition *Pokémon* cards I could get my hands on. Not only did these cards have the first-edition stamp on them, there were also theme decks and starter decks. I bought all I could and put them away for later.

A month after this, the regular edition of *Pokémon* cards arrived. These were printed in much higher quantities, and I received twelve cases this time around. Most card and comic stores sold the packs for $5 to $8 each, and up to $12 in malls. I stuck with the suggested retail price of $3.99 and sold out within a few weeks.

Since it was so much like *Magic*, I was perfectly positioned to become a premier *Pokémon* seller. I had singles in display cases and taught kids how to play the game. I also introduced a promotion offering $10 in store credit to anyone who could beat me in a best-of-three *Pokémon* match. I rarely had to give out a credit voucher at first. As an adult with access to an unlimited supply of cards, I did have a big advantage. But I had to end the promotion once too many kids started to win.

With my well-established *Magic* tournaments, adding *Pokémon* tournaments was an obvious move. They quickly became so popular that my store was too small to hold everyone who wanted to play. I was able to expand the store a little bit and also moved into an adjoining apartment at the same time. Additionally, I started running two tournaments per week, for kids 13 and under on Mondays and for 16 and under onWedensdays. No adults in these tournaments – I wanted to keep *Pokémon* just for the kids.

I always ran fair tournaments, and gave out the best prizes possible while still making a profit. I charged $10 to play and awarded prizes to the top eight players, which was usually around half of the turnout. The prizes depended on the number of players – the better the crowd, the better the prizes.

One prize that was always sure to attract many players was a Charizard card. Charizard was one of the first holographic *Pokémon* cards. Holographic cards were the rarest in the game and all highly valued. While no rarer than any of the other holographic cards in the set, Charizard was the one everybody wanted. Each box included a few of those holographic cards, so they weren't too hard for me to come by. But I never had a problem selling them.

Most stores were selling regular-edition Charizards for $35 to $50, but I always sold mine for $25. Not a day went by that I didn't sell one. I had a list of over 100 people who wanted Charizards, and I promised them all that I would sell them one for $25 before Christmas of 1999. And I kept that promise – I sold a Charizard to each and every one of them.

It is not too hard to see why Charizard was so loved. First of all, he is a big, fire-breathing dragon. In the original Pokémon games for Gameboy, you get to choose between three different Pokémon that will accompany you and evolve through your journey. Charizard is the final evolution of one of those starter Pokémon, Charmander. That meant that roughly one third of players of that game ended up with a Charizard. But it was likely far more than a third, as Charizard was also on the cover art for the red version of the Gameboy game. Charizard was perhaps the most iconic Pokémon when it first debut, and having a Charizard card was a status symbol for Pokémon fans of all kinds.

For the most serious collectors, just any Charizard wasn't enough. You see, when the base set of Pokémon cards first came out, the initial print run were all stamped with a small "first edition" insignia. This drove up the value of any first edition compared to the regular version. First edition Charizards went for $300 and I couldn't keep them in stock. The first edition stamping continued on future Pokémon set for years, but the first edition Charizard was, and still is, the most sought-after Pokémon card of all time.

New expansion sets for *Pokémon* came out every few months. These cards sold just as well as the original ones for the first year and a half. I always sold out quickly, offering the packs at the suggested retail price. While there was never another Charizard, the holographic cards always fetched a few bucks.

Theme decks also sold well. These were aimed at newer players and came with the rulebook and everything you needed to start playing. Each one included a good holographic card, which made them desirable to players at all skill levels.

One day at Marshall's Creek, a guy came by my booth to see if I wanted to buy some holographic cards. He had 500 each of Gyarados, Mewtwo, Ninetales, and Hitmonchan, all base deck holos. It was unbelievable to see 2000 mint condition holographic cards. The prospective seller said he came to me first. This was no surprise, as I was on the front row and had a large vinyl "Beanie Babies & Pokémon" banner flying high in the air over my booth, visible from anywhere in the market.

He asked me how many cards I wanted. I said that I wanted all of them, or none. I knew it would kill the prices if everyone at this market had some of these, since there were about 30 other dealers who had recently jumped into *Pokémon*. I offered him $2000. He hesitated at first, but settled on $2500 cash for all of them.

When I bought this trove of holos, they were going for $8 to $10 each. I dropped the price down to $5 apiece, the lowest price anywhere around, but I made sure to keep just one or two in my display case at a time. They sold steadily, and eventually I sold them all at the $5 price.

The same guy came back to me at the market again three months later when the next wave of theme decks was released. I bought another 2000 holographic cards from him, this time getting Khangaskhan, Lapras, Vaporean, and Muk from the Fossil and Jungle decks. They didn't sell as well as the first wave, and I eventually dropped the price to $3 each. But if I had these cards today they would be worth quite a small fortune.

I later learned that a factory in Pennsylvania had been contracted to print those theme decks and realized that the cards I bought had probably been stolen by an employee. But that's why sometimes you can't ask too many questions when you come across a deal too good to be true.

I was not selling video games when *Pokémon Red* and *Blue* came out, but I had set up an account with Nintendo by the time the next version was announced. Instead of a whole new game, Nintendo released *Pokémon Yellow*. This updated version allowed players to have a Pikachu, arguably the most popular Pokémon, follow them around in the game.

I ordered 500 copies of *Pokémon Yellow,* anticipating my order being cut short. They cost $29 each, with a retail price of $35. I had a mild panic when I received all 500 copies. Besides eating up more of my cash than I had planned, I saw that Walmart was selling the game for $30! I was afraid I was going to get stuck with a massive pile of *Pokémon Yellow* that I would end up selling at a loss. Luckily, all the big stores sold out quickly, and I was able to sell all of mine at $35 after all.

Between 1998 and 1999, there was overwhelming demand for just about every *Pokémon* toy that came out. I could go to Toys "R" Us or Walmart, pay the full retail price, and *still* make money. One example of this was the Pokédex, an electronic device that contained a catalog of all the Pokémon – you just typed in a name and a picture of that Pokémon popped up, along with all the information about it. These retailed for $30 but were so scarce that they easily resold at flea markets for $75.

Never mind catching these critters – you couldn't get away from them! If you went to a mall, you were surrounded by Pokémon everywhere you turned. At the mania's height, a Pokémon-branded store opened in New York City. It carried only Pokémon merchandise, with many items exclusive to that store. There was even a contest with a special Pikachu VW Beetle as the grand prize.

Burger King offered a line of Pokéballs that came with a gold Pokémon card inside. Like McDonald's Teenie Beanies, these were in extremely high demand and sold briskly on the secondary market. Topps, the sports card manufacturer, released a set of *Pokémon* trading cards. While not as insanely popular as the card game, these were still highly coveted by children and adults alike.

At one point a poster came out that showed all 151 original Pokémon. I carried them in my store, even though they were being sold everywhere, and priced them at $5 instead of the $7.99 retail price. I went through ten racks of that poster, making a lot of kids happy along the way, while making $1 per poster myself.

Pokémon: The First Movie was released in theaters in 1999. Each ticket came with a random special promo card with a gold stamp on it. There were four cards: Pikachu, Electabuzz, Dragonair, and Mewtwo. I went to opening night and was happy to see the local theater filled with my customers. A few days later, a manager from that same movie theater brought in a case of 600 cards. At $900 for the case, they cost me $1.50 each and sold very well at $5.

Pokémon: The Movie 2000 arrived the next year with another special promo card: an Ancient Mew. Looking like an ancient Egyptian version of a *Pokémon* card, it was purple, shiny, and super hot, selling for $10. Unfortunately, too many were produced, and the price eventually dropped to a dollar.

Promo cards appeared everywhere after that. They were included with video games, toys, magazines, and more. There was even a calendar that came with a special Pikachu card that was more powerful when you played it on your birthday! When Toys "R" Us started running *Pokémon* tournaments in their stores, they gave out a special promo Mew to everyone who came to play. While their tournaments soon fizzled out, Toys "R" Us initially was able to get thousands of kids to show up for that Mew.

When *Pokémon* first arrived, it looked like just one more in a seemingly endless string of consumer crazes. But its impact was so big that it survived the eventual collapse that plagued almost every 90s fad. The characters made an indelible imprint on a generation, rebounding in popularity in the 2000s and 2010s. Today *Pokémon* remains a healthy franchise that retains its old fans while adding new ones.

Chapter 19

1998 was the peak year in a decade obsessed with buying the next hot thing. Pokémon and Beanie Babies were at their height, but a slew of other products made their marks as well. One such item had been around since 500 BC, yet never saw more popularity than it did in 1998.

I am talking, about yo-yos. This simple toy is composed of some string and a wooden or plastic wheel. They have gone in and out of fashion through the centuries, but had been steadily growing in popularity in America since the 1960s. A company called Yomega began marketing a new type of high performance yo-yo in the 1980s, but I did not hear of them until 1998, when they seemed to catch on with kids everywhere in an instant.

Whenever I got two requests on the same day for an unfamiliar product, I tracked that item down no matter what. One day two kids asked about Yomega yo-yos, so I looked up the company and set up an account that day. The two best sellers were the Brain and the Fireball. They sold for about $8 each, and soon I was selling 20 to 30 per week!

I eventually carried the full Yomega line, but only the Brain and the Fireball sold like crazy. One high-end model had a $90 retail price, and I sold the six I had ordered. I sold just about every yo-yo I had when I brought them to the flea market for the first time. When I walked around the market later that day, I saw kids playing with yo-yos everywhere.

Within a few weeks, it seemed like half the vendors in the market had yo-yos in their setup. The fad did not stick for long, and yo-yos were soon relegated back to a novelty toy. Along the way I relearned how to use yo-yos myself after not touching one since my own childhood. I must admit that the Yomegas were infinitely better than the ones I had as a kid.

1998 was also a big year for the Spice Girls. This all-female pop group formed in 1994, but 1998 was the biggest year for their merchandise. Up to this point, both the store and my flea market setup primarily attracted male customers. *Pokémon* brought in some girls, but the Spice Girls gear really diversified my demographic.

One day someone stopped by my flea market booth and tried to sell me pink "GIRL POWER" lanyards for $2 each. I bargained him down to $1 each and bought all 200. I was a little nervous — I knew the Spice Girls were popular, but this item didn't say anything about them specifically. I priced the lanyards at $5 each and hung a bunch in the very front of my booth. Two tween girls noticed them a few minutes later, and each bought one. By the end of the day, I had sold 15 lanyards and was no longer worried. My only concern at that point was securing some real Spice Girls products.

I bought some Spice Girls posters, which had a retail price of $8 each. I sold them at the markets and in my store for $5 apiece and went through several racks of posters every week for the next few months. I was also able to find Spice Girls trading cards. Although they were much larger than typical trading cards, they sold well. But the best item of all was the Spice Girls dolls.

While the dolls had a retail price of $10.99, they fetched much higher amounts at the flea markets. They flew out of my booth at $20, and I was able to get $30 for the Scary Spice dolls as they were limited to one per case. After setting up at a collectibles show at Freehold Mall one day, I walked down to Toys "R" Us and discovered that they had just restocked their Spice Girls dolls for the weekend. I filled a shopping cart with all they had. They were my best sellers that weekend, and I had none left to bring back to my store.

Spice Girls dolls were just one of many toys that sent me running to big box stores every morning before my own store opened, checking for a rotating cast of products that I could resell. Furby was another 1998 toy that every parent was trying to find. This furry electronic toy captured hearts and wallets by looking cute and speaking a gibberish language called "Furbish".

Furbys were advertised as a wonder toy with multiple amazing abilities, but they didn't really live up to their hype. They were still highly coveted by children as well as adult collectors, because they came in all sorts of colors and designs, with some combinations being rarer and more desirable than others. Furbys retailed for $35, but I was able to sell them for $95 – and I usually had the lowest price at the markets!

When stores had Furbys in stock, they usually limited purchases to two per customer. I returned daily to try to pick up a pair, and usually they were gone by the time I came back the next day. There was a Caldor's department store where I never had any luck, but I kept stopping by out of habit. To my surprise, one day I stumbled upon a display of about forty Furbys there. There was no limit posted, so I filled two shopping carts, paid in cash, and was on my way. I was used to getting one or two at a time, so that was a gold mine.

About a week before Christmas, I stopped by a Toys "R" Us on the way to my regular Beanie buying rendezvous. They had a display of almost 500 Furbys, along with the dreaded "Two per customer" sign. I bought two. At that time I had long hair, so I tucked it into the back of my shirt and went back for two more. I was wearing a reversible jacket, so I reversed it in the parking lot, put on a hat, and bought another two.

I was out of quick disguise options, but I thought I might be able to score a few more toys. I stood outside the store and asked everyone that came in if they were buying any Furbys. If they said they weren't, I offered them $100 to buy two for me. The two Furbys rang up for $74.20 at the cash register. I told them to keep the change and just give me the Furbys on their way out.

Several people took me up on the deal. One lady even suggested having her three children go in one at a time. I was able to get 72 Furbys before the store manager called the police on me. I told the cop the truth about what I was doing, and he just told me to leave.

For a time, Furbys were worth their weight in gold. Several different waves were released, along with a few limited editions that brought big bucks. They were the hot item of Christmas 1998, and kids still wanted them as 1999 began. But this did not last long.

Chapter 20

    1999 was the last year of a decade, a century, and a millennium, but it didn't feel any different at the start. Beanie Babies and Pokémon dominated sales, while *Magic* tournaments still brought a good turnout. Even when a dedicated Beanie Baby store opened in Hackettstown, I was able to beat their prices and keep the cash flowing.

    This was all about to change, and there were warning signs. Fads come and go, but when long-established industries started to fall, it was the beginning of the end. By 1999 the comic book industry had collapsed, and I even stopped carrying new release comic books.

    The comic book speculation market reached its saturation point some time in 1995. New comic book stores were still opening, but more were closing, and the comic book publishers followed. Within a few years, most of the indie upstart publishers were out of business. Even Marvel, recently at the very top of the industry, filed for bankruptcy in 1997.

    While many things contributed to Marvel's downfall, I believe that the biggest factor was their decision to switch to self-distributing. They made this move right at the peak of the comic boom, and it backfired on them as the market came crashing down. Marvel got stuck with massive printings of "collectible" issues that were no longer in high demand, and they couldn't even cover the cost of their distribution service.

Marvel was able to continue publishing, and eventually rebounded stronger than ever before, but at the time their tragic downfall was an ominous sign. The vast majority of comic book buyers in the 90s were speculators who were in it to make money. As soon as the market faltered, most of them stopped buying and tried to sell off what they had. And like dominoes, as soon as one did it, everyone was getting out.

However, they soon found that their hoarded books had no value. Since all these speculators had large quantities of the same handful of books, such as "The Death of Superman," there were dozens of others trying to sell stacks of the same thing. And no one was buying.

"The Death of Superman" and similar well-hyped "event" stories all turned out to be big gimmicks with no apparent long-term significance. People thought Superman was really gone for good, but he returned within a year. Batman healed and was back at full strength in time for the next big thing. Valiant had saturated the market to the point that no one even wanted the older, rarer books. Fans lost interest in Image's forgettable stories and cookie-cutter characters, and that company fell off the radar for years. And Marvel was the worst offender of all, pumping out an endless stream of books with flashy covers and no substance.

Instead of learning their lesson, most of the comic book speculators made the same mistake with Beanie Babies and Pokémon. While these stayed hot for a few years longer, they had also peaked, though Beanie Babies managed to stay strong right up to the end of the millennium.

Somewhat ironically, the last Beanie Babies that drew any kind of demand were the Year 2000 Beanies. This line of Beanies, mostly teddy bears, came out at the end of 1999. While they did sell above retail at first, they did not fetch as much as previous new releases had, and the prices dropped off steeply soon after release. I had probably made more money on Beanies than any other item, but I took this as a clear sign that they were at the end of their time.

In January of 2000, a woman came into my store looking to sell her Beanie collection. I offered her $1700 and she didn't take it. A year later, she came back, hoping to get the same deal. But it was too late as the Beanie boom was over, and the Beanie bust had arrived. I offered her $400 and she took it. She was smart, because if she had waited another year I probably might have only offered her $40.

Before long, people were coming into my store every day to try to sell their collections. Most were offended by the prices I offered. Even though they knew that Beanies were dropping in value, they didn't realize how bad it was. I did, but I also knew that just because Beanie Babies were out of fashion, that didn't mean they were completely worthless.

I continued to do flea markets for several years after the Beanie crash, and Beanies remained a strong seller at $3 each during that time. I purchased collections at a buck a Beanie, even once-hot Beanies like Princess. As much as people had wanted Beanies, now they wanted to get rid of them just as badly.

I bought so many Beanies at $1 each that I was getting buried in them. I had to stop buying, and after a while I had to lower my selling price to $2. Finally, I dropped the price to $1 and blew out the last few hundred I had. By that time bulk collections were selling for around 25 cents apiece! There were pages and pages on eBay of people desperately trying to get anything they could for their collections.

Though it hurt me to think back on her former worth, I even let Princess go at $3. Still, while they no longer brought in the big bucks, Beanies were a consistent seller for me from the day I bought a table full of them, down to the very end. Other than the prices, the only thing that changed were the customers. Beanies were no longer coveted by middle-aged, middle-class women. No, most of the Beanies I sold during that final period went to the customer they were actually intended for: children.

Chapter 21

By mid-2000, sales in my store were dropping steadily, and regular markets and shows were starting to disappear. I had gotten farther in this business than I ever thought. I knew things were shifting, but I didn't know what came next. Was I supposed to fight to stay open as long as possible?

I had originally liked being in business for myself because I made my own rules. Now I found myself locked into a routine while the world was changing around me. My store lease ended in February 2001, and I thought long and hard about whether to stay in business.

By this time, I was really only selling to a core group of regular customers. *Magic* and *Pokémon* tournaments continued to bring in the dedicated players. The comic book store in town closed, so I started selling new comics again. It was nice to see that the companies had learned a few lessons from the bust and were focusing on quality stories without too many gimmicks and fancy covers.

I also had four or five guys who still bought sports card packs regularly. Sports cards are a very odd commodity. After dealing with them for over a decade, I came to the conclusion that some sports card buyers actually have gambling addictions. They are forever chasing the thrill of opening a $5 pack and finding a card that sells for $500.

The customer who had been buying from me the longest was an iron worker named Barry. He lived in the Poconos and bought packs of cards from me at Marshall's Creek for many years. He worked in northern New Jersey, so he became a regular at my store as well and stopped by on his way home from work.

Barry would drop a couple hundred bucks a week on packs of cards. He always opened the packs right then and there, as soon as he paid for them. His hands shook in anticipation. Sometimes he got very lucky, but he'd never sell them. When he pulled a "hot" card, I always offered to sell it for him, telling him it would only drop in value if he waited too long. He always turned me down and hung onto the cards.

One time Barry pulled a Rickey Williams autographed rookie card from a Topps football pack. I could have gotten him $500 for it, but he was not interested. Yet at one point he told me that he was spending too much money on cards and asked if I would accept grams of silver in trade! He had previously been a silver collector and had hundreds of one-gram bars. I offered $5 in trade for each bar, which was fair market value. He took it all in packs over the months that followed.

Barry found eBay in 2000. His problem remained the same, only he did his business online. eBay was, and still is, the marketplace of the 21st century. You don't even have to pay for gas and spend time digging through a booth or a store to buy whatever you want – you don't even have to leave your couch! Understandably, I started losing more customers every day to the internet.

Walmart's arrival was another blow. Everyone in Hackettstown was thrilled when Walmart opened there in 1999. Not me. I had to go there every day, either buying them out of the items we both sold, or lowering my prices to beat theirs. Competing with them wasn't my biggest concern, but keeping up with their stock was.

Once the big box stores like Walmart and Toys "R" Us started carrying something I sold, I could still beat or at least match their price, but I barely made a profit. Even worse, my customers shopped at Walmart for plenty of other stuff, and often ended up buying items there that they normally bought from me. Since they didn't have to go out of their way to make an extra stop at my store, they saved time even if they didn't save any money.

Between the internet, which was growing more relevant every day in 2000, and the Walmart, which was not going anywhere, it was hard to keep my customers. The manufacturers piled on as well, changing their policies and raising their minimum purchase requirements, making it very difficult for a little operation like mine to keep an account with them. They preferred the simplicity and huge paychecks from the big box stores, eventually making it nearly impossible for anyone else to buy direct from them.

While my store was surviving on the strength of regular customers, it had always been more of a supplement to the flea markets and shows. Some of the well-established flea markets, which had been around before any of the wild 90s crazes hit, were still around. These remained good for the time being, but the card and comic shows were a different story.

While I spent much of the 1990s buying and selling at shows nearly every day, by 2000 my only show was the Tuesday night one in Parsippany. This was a shell of what it used to be, however, with attendance way down. In 1998, all 50 dealer tables were rented and at least 500 people paid the $2 entrance fee every week. By the end of 2000, less than half the dealer tables were full, with 100 attendees on a good night. And those numbers were continuing to decline.

Life as I knew it had changed seemingly overnight. For over a decade, I had been riding the wave from one hot product to the next. Suddenly there was no hot product anymore, at least not anything I sold. Collecting had soured for many people, and the hot new trends were all technology. Video games were moving into the mainstream, people were running out to buy computers, and soon everyone would have a cell phone.

Most store owners in my position were trying to adapt to the new times. They either created an online selling presence in addition to their shops, moved entirely online, or went out of business altogether. Since I was still doing flea markets, I did not really want to spread myself too thin. On the other hand, I had a few reasons to try to stay open. It was good outlet for the local kids. The *Magic* and *Pokémon* tournaments were fun for them in a town without much other kid-friendly entertainment. Ultimately, however, my decision on the fate of the store rested on my biggest priority: my own kid.

My son, James, was born in July 1991, during the final throes of my transition from tie-dyes to comics and cards. I remember reading the latest issue of *Punisher* while I waited for him to be born. Entitled "Maternity War", the cover featured the Punisher holding several newborns while shooting machine guns. This freaked me out a bit, as I was reading it in an actual maternity ward, but I had no need to worry. James was a healthy and happy infant, with no machine guns required.

As a baby, every outfit James wore was tie-dyed. Earlier, I mentioned the tie-dye Batman onesies that I sold. Well, I had made the first one for James. When I saw how good it looked on him, I decided to start making it in all sizes. He spent many a day in a playpen in the back of my booth, a walking billboard for my baby gear.

James arrived at the perfect time to catch the collector wave of the 90s. This meant he had first access to everything a kid could want. Many of the kids from his school came to my store, but whatever they wanted, James had first whether he wanted it or not.

Just like me in my grandfather's store, my son had an endless supply of comics to read. He loved them even before he could recognize words, and they helped him learn to read. Over the years he read both classic and current comics, as many as a kid could want.

James took to *Magic* the same way. At first he created his own rules based on the art. Once he was able to read, he picked up the game very quickly. By the time the *Pokémon* card game came along, he was already a seasoned *Magic* player. James played in the older age bracket on both games, even when he was under ten.

His bed held an impressive selection of Beanie Babies. When the *Pokémon* cartoon first came out, I had to convince him to give it a try. At the age of seven, he thought it was too childish. He finally gave in to its allure after I had him sit down and watch an episode.

As soon as James could talk, I gave him opportunities to make money for himself. I paid him a small salary to help around the store. When he came with me to a flea market or a show, I paid him some cash along with something from my booth or a toy from the market.

The summer he turned eight, James took some cash he had saved up and opened his own business: James' Novelties. He got the bottom half of an eight-foot table in a prime position near the front door of my store. This meant it was at a child's eye level, and he knew what his peers wanted. He picked out all the merchandise himself from the Rhode Island Novelty wholesale catalog.

I believe he got the idea for his own store when I received a copy of the Rhode Island catalog but did not want to order anything. Most of the goods retailed for less than a dollar, so I didn't think it was worth the time to go through the thousands of products in their huge catalog.

James had just been sitting around the store that summer, so he had plenty of time to browse the catalog, and I gave him full control. He picked out everything himself, restocked as needed, and kept all the money he made. James' Novelties sold all kinds of cheap playthings that his peers enjoyed. There were superballs, whoopie cushions, sticky hands, keychains, fortune telling fish, and much, much more.

He made smart selections based on his own tastes. At that time, items with a green alien motif were popular, and these became a staple of his setup. As his business grew, he even added a few higher-priced items such as inflatable green aliens. There was a hamburger yo-yo that sold for around 50 cents. When the yo-yo craze hit, he doubled the price and put them front and center in his display. That summer, it was hard to keep the hamburger yo-yo's in stock, and James made a lot of cash as a result.

The store was a great place for James when he was young, since he had access to anything a kid could ever want. He loved Lego, and at one point he was so into it that I started carrying Lego in the store just so he could order all he wanted at cost. But while the store itself was good for him, our town in New Jersey was not.

Hackettstown was home to the Mars candy factory, manufacturing M&Ms and other sweets. Most people who lived in the town worked there, but we really only knew people through our store. I still had some friends in New Paltz and sometimes went on trips there with James, which we enjoyed.

By 2000, James was getting older, and soon would not care so much about Lego or *Pokémon* tournaments. With the store's lease renewal deadline approaching, I made my decision. We were going to move back to New Paltz.

New Paltz had grown since I moved away. The mountains and the college attracted more people every year. The town was lively, with new businesses springing up on the main street. It was a wonderful thing to see.

We moved to New Paltz before the official closing of the store, and I bounced back and forth for a while. The final closing of my shop was definitely a little sad, but unceremonious. Most of my customers had moved on and it was time for me to do the same. I knew I was making the right move for us, but I wasn't quite sure how it'd play out. I still had some flea markets to rely on, but other than that it was gonna be tough.

Chapter 22

In my head, I had always planned on opening another store in New Paltz. The old comic shop I used to buy from was still there, but they didn't sell *Magic*. I knew I could get a tournament scene going and eke out a living, if not a booming business. I probably should have tried to open one right away, but instead I did the same thing everyone else in my position did. I turned to the internet.

I jumped right into eBay as soon as I closed my store in February 2001. I had never even used a computer before. Despite a steep learning curve, I taught myself everything I needed to know to become an eBay seller. The first thing I sold was a *Sports Illustrated* #1 that had been hanging in my store for years. I only got $52 for it but it was a start.

On eBay, I sold the same way I did at a flea market, with a little bit of everything. I sold sports cards and *Magic* and *Pokémon* singles. I dabbled in stamp and coin collections, wargames, action figures, and even bought and sold a 1977 Pontiac Trans Am. Years later, I realized that if I had specialized in one thing, such as *Magic*, I might have had an early e-commerce website and evolved into the future.

But eBay did pretty well for me, and I soon became a PowerSeller. In a strange twist of fate, I sold to some of the people who had been customers in my store, including Blam and Barry, the iron worker. Between eBay and flea markets, it seemed to be enough. I picked up flea market items to flip on eBay, and bought products on eBay to sell at the markets.

After closing the store, a few more trends came along to keep me alive at the flea markets. Though none quite reached the heights of the 90s, a couple of these were crazes in their own rights. The first of these, Razor scooters, came out in 1999, but didn't become popular until a year later, when my store was in in its final days. For a year or so after that, it was a great item at flea markets.

Toys "R" Us had Razor scooters for $99 and was selling out left and right. I had a great spot at Marshall's Creek, and I was approached by someone who wanted me to sell Razor Scooters for him. He wanted $75 each. I agreed and put them out for $95. He dropped off a load of 30 scooters every Saturday and returned for the cash on Sunday night. On a good weekend they'd all be gone by the time he came to collect. This deal went on all summer, after which Razor Scooters dipped out of the public eye.

Probably the hottest product after I closed the store was *Yu-Gi-Oh*. This franchise is very similar to Pokémon, with an animated show and trading card game at the core, but targeted at a slightly older crowd. The cards were cooler, with intimidating monsters and more complex rules. If I still had a store, *Yu-Gi-Oh* tournaments would no doubt have been very popular for me.

Despite not having the space to run *Yu-Gi-Oh* tournaments, I had some good success selling the cards. I sold packs at flea markets and on eBay. I also sold singles in the early days. These were very popular since there weren't very many stores selling singles anymore. The internet eventually got flooded with them, but for the first five or six *Yu-Gi-Oh* sets I did very well.

Shortly after *Yu-Gi-Oh* hit the US, another type of product from Japan became popular: blind box packaging. These were collectibles, often figures or statuettes, that came sealed in opaque packages. The thrill was in opening them to find out what you would get.

Anything with blind box packaging was hot for a few months. One example was Bearbricks. These were little plastic teddy bear figures with different colors and designs. Multiple series were produced, and each series had a rare bear. People went crazy over these things, but not for long.

Less than a year after closing my store, my flea market setup had inherited a new generation of products. Next to the $3 Beanie table and the packs of sports cards were *Yu-Gi-Oh* and Razor scooters. People still came to flea markets for this kind of stuff, and my business was growing online. Despite not finding a store, I was doing okay. Store rents were very high in New Paltz and there just wasn't any really hot item to build a new store around.

After the hype for these few successful new products died down, I stumbled to find something else I could lean on. Celebrations of the new millennium did not last long. After 9/11, perhaps the greatest tragedy America has ever faced, the national mindset shifted. People did not care about frivolities like collecting children's toys anymore.

I tried to shift my business to match the desires of American consumers, with mixed success. I started selling personal security equipment like hidden cameras and tasers, along with camouflage clothing and survival gear. These sold decently, but I did not like it. I had always focused on stuff that was fun, light-hearted, and mostly for kids. But it was not kids that bought these items. They did not mix well with the other stuff in my booth, and I soon replaced the personal security equipment with more comic books.

The last hot item I carried was Homies. They were little figurines of Latino people that sold in vending machines for 50 cents. I was able to get them in bags of 100 from the company that supplied the machines. Homies were selling online by the set, and generated significant interest for a while. One of the steadiest flea markets that I was still vending at, in Fishkill, New York, attracted a huge Latino community that loved Homies, buying them by the handful. I had Homies in a large bowl and charged 50¢, same as vending machines. People loved that they could pick the ones they wanted, instead of buying them at random from the vending machines.

I paid a quarter per Homie, and I went through about 5000 each of the first eight series. Some other products came out, like the more expensive Homies in vehicles, but they did not last long. Still, my profits of a quarter apiece added up to some real money. But in the end, Homies were the last new product to ever join my setup.

Flea markets were my final holdout from the old days. When these started drying up, I had to accept that my time in this business might be finished. Making a quarter at a time is no way to make a living, even selling 5000 of something. I became a full-time eBayer and did markets for as long as possible.

When a few more of the staple markets closed, so did my business. At the end, all I had left was the Fishkill flea market on Sundays. I didn't start doing this until after my store closed, so I had not seen it at its peak. It was decent for a while but after a couple years the attendance had dwindled. The market took place in the parking lot of an abandoned mall. There was talk of another mall coming in, which would put an end to the flea market. I stopped vending before I saw how that turned out.

Converting to an entirely eBay-based living was not an easy transition for me at first. I had always been a slow adopter of new technology. Just as I had been one of the last stores with a credit card machine, by the time I started selling online, many other card and comic sellers had already established a foothold in this new market. But with time, I was able to carve out a space of my own on eBay. After a few months without doing a market, I had to admit that there were some advantages to the digital marketplace.

On eBay, I never had to worry about a rainstorm popping up out of the blue, as happened often at the Swap Shop in Florida. It might pour down rain for ten minutes and then return to sunshine like nothing happened – except that anything uncovered in my setup was drenched. Like many markets, the Swap Shop had indoor spaces available, but I always chose an outdoor spot. On beautiful days, which is when you could really make a fortune at flea markets, nobody wants to be indoors.

When my whole living was based on outdoor vending, I was a slave to the weather. But unless the forecast predicted 100% chance of rain, I gave it a try. On rainy days I could still make about a third of what I made on a normal day, which was better than nothing. I had to cut my set-up down to just the best stuff and leave room under the tarp for customers to keep dry. If they were there to buy, I would stay to sell. But that meant suffering through rain, snow, sleet, hail, and worst of all, wind.

Not only did the wind blow merchandise every which way, on a bad day it could flip your canopy right over. One nasty, rainy day at a festival in Hoboken, NJ, a huge gust of wind whooshed through the market. I watched an entire row of tents across from me go flying into the Hudson River. Thankfully, my canopy was bungee-corded to my truck *and* staked to the ground, and it held on.

I was in the Poconos for the one time my booth didn't hold up. It wasn't raining hard, but it was enough to send people without canopies home. I had a 20' x 10' booth and removed the tarp from half of it to let air flow through, then attached it to stakes that I drove into the concrete. I thought that should've been secure enough, but I was wrong – the wind flipped the whole thing a few minutes later. Fortunately, no one got hurt and I only lost a little bit of merchandise.

Weather wasn't the only thing taking products from me. I've always had to fight theft, from cops "confiscating" stacks of tie-dyes to teenagers trying to walk out of my store with a box of the latest *Magic* set. When it was the latter, they never got far.

One time as I was packing up my booth, I heard a popping sound. Someone had used a knife to force the lock on a jewelry case and stole a Michael Jordan rookie. I was asking $450 for that card. Out of the corner of my eye, I saw a teenager scoot out of my booth. I chased him down, retrieved the card, and gave him a hard kick in the butt.

Another time, a different teen asked me what the most expensive comic I had for sale was. I pointed to an early *Spider-Man* I had out for $400. A minute later it was gone. I followed the kid out of the booth and grabbed his bag, which was full of comic books. I took that and the $80 he had on him. I told him that if he wanted his money or his comics, he needed to come back with a cop or a parent. I gave him a swift kick in the butt as well, and never saw him again.

On eBay, there are no butts to kick. There is no more flea market justice. With credit cards and automated payments, no one can pull a fast one on you and steal something. On rainy days, you can sip tea in the warmth of your home and still make money. And that's just what I did for a while.

What I didn't even realize was that I was using a bottom of the line computer, connecting to the internet through a dial-up modem, and spending hours online to make very little. Competition was endless and everyone was fighting to have the lowest price. So while I sold plenty of stuff it just didn't add up to much, if any, profit. In reality I was probably making only $5 an hour, if I was lucky.

My life turned into a cycle of answering emails, stuffing envelopes and boxes, and running to the post office. I had gone from roaming the parking lots of Dead shows to sitting on my couch. It was business as usual for a couple of years. There were no wild deals, no hilarious moments, and no huge profits. I was still living off the high times of the 90s.

In the end, I sold off everything I had on eBay. After more than a decade of self-employment, I had to go find a "real" job again. The last time I had applied for a job was at Not Fade Away, my first step into the world of tie-dyes. With a gap of well over ten years in my resume, I knew my next job would not be so colorful.

Inspired by a silly episode of *King of Queens*, I decided that my new career was going to be bartending. It was not necessarily the smartest choice, but it didn't require a college degree, and it seemed like a cool job for a guy in my position, turning forty years old.

I continued to sell on eBay during the job search, and kept it as a side business even after I had a new job. In the end, it became more hassle than it was worth. I still enjoy reading comic books, and I still have my eBay account, but I don't sell much anymore. (The name is futureseer – look me up sometime, I always have something!)

As for tending bar, I got off to a rocky start. I had a few fun jobs that didn't pay enough at first, but eventually attained steady employment. Working as a bartender full time for over a decade, people at bars often asked me my story. And basically what I'd tell them was one of the stories you just read. Sometimes they would tell me I should write a book. Well, here it is.

Epilogue

The 1990s came and went, but nothing ever truly goes away, especially in today's digital world. The internet helps even the smallest of niches continue to find its buyers. And almost two decades into this millennium, nearly every product that was popular in the 90s lives on today. Without question, the mania for those items will never again return to the heights of that decadent decade but, for better or worse, everything from that era has simply been absorbed into our culture.

Take the humble tie-dye, for example. When I began making and selling tie-dyes, they were exclusively produced by hippies. However, their origins in communes were soon obscured, if not completely forgotten. As soon as companies like Not Fade Away started making tie-dyes in bulk, they became a commodity. And true to their name, Not Fade Away did not fade away, and still maintain a bustling business at their store in Woodstock.

Not Fade Away's biggest competitor during the late 80s was a company called Liquid Blue. Their shirts had much more subdued colors and simpler patterns but used amazing silk screens over the tie dye. Seeing the two next to each other, the difference was instantly noticeable. Liquid Blue's style became quite popular, and they remain one of the biggest manufacturers of tie-dyes.

I began buying from Liquid Blue during my my last year of vending on the Dead tour. They had a line of eye-catching shirts featuring New Age and space themes. Those shirts were more like wearable art. By the time I opened my store, Liquid Blue shirts were the only tie-dyed gear that I still sold. They eventually moved into licensed products, including *Star Wars*, and their shirts sold well for me throughout the 90s.

Liquid Blue had a license for Grateful Dead-related merchandise. They combined that with good business sense to cash in on the Beanie Baby craze by producing a Beanie-style line of Grateful Dead dancing bears. These were about the size of a Ty Beanie, with each one featuring a different color pattern and a Grateful Dead song title on their name tags. I was very glad that I had continued selling their shirts, as that got me in on the ground floor with those bears. I sold several hundred at the markets.

The original tie-dyes were hand-made products, and no two were exactly alike. Did it matter that Liquid Blue's products were mass produced, featuring nearly identical designs? Ultimately, no. Once tie-dyes became mainstream, minor details like craftsmanship and individuality became irrelevant. This is not to say that Liquid Blue does not produce high-quality products. I would not have continued carrying their stuff if they weren't. But their process is a far cry from one guy in a studio apartment, doing everything by hand.

Tie-dyes have earned their place in society now. Long synonymous with the counterculture, they still seem to be the go-to expression of kinship with the hippies of yore. The Grateful Dead disbanded years ago, but the surviving members continue to play on in many forms, including a new band called Dead & Company. Their shows capture much of what made the Dead tour so interesting. There are still plenty of vendors on Shakedown Street, including a few old Deadheads trying to make a buck by selling handcrafted tie-dyes. The only difference is that now they must compete with the world of the internet.

While it may seem sad to see a once-counterculture item become utterly mainstream, it is ultimately a good thing. The companies that could adapt, like Liquid Blue, survived and prospered, and are now doing better than ever. And, as you will see, this same "adapt or die" concept applies to any product of the 90s.

One industry that nearly died out entirely was sports cards. Sports cards have a history that goes back to the early 20th century, but for decades they appealed only to kids and a tiny group of adult collectors. When they started catching on with a wider audience in the late 1980s, card manufacturers changed their business practices to capitalize on the newfound interest. This generally meant making fancier types of cards that sold for more money. Within a few years, the average sports cards were worthless. Collectors only cared about the premium cards.

For decades, sports cards had remained essentially the same. The typical card featured a photo of the player on the front, and their statistics and other information on the back. The 90s saw waves of evolution in the basic card, with higher-quality cardstock and die cut designs. The manufacturers had even more success when they began randomly adding rare insert cards in the sealed packs, a trend that grew throughout the 90s. Soon holographic, foil, and dozens of other gimmicky card types became the main draw of sports cards.

The introduction of autographed cards was even more noteworthy. When you could have a card that a favorite player had actually signed – individually, by hand – who wanted a card with a mere photo? Autographed cards were a huge success, and every card company worth their salt in the 90s had randomly inserted autographs.

Then came game-used memorabilia cards. These cards featured a small square containing a tiny portion of some piece of equipment that had been used in a professional sporting event. The most common held pieces of a player's jersey, though there were plenty of other things you could find stuck on a card, like a chip of leather from a game-used ball, or dirt from the batter's box. This trend started in 1996 with the "Burning Rubber" cards featuring pieces of a tire that had actually been used in a NASCAR race. The novelty of these cards drew attention from established collectors and new fans alike. Like everything in the 90s, once a gimmick took off, every other company jumped in and overloaded the market with imitations.

By the end of the 90s, autograph and memorabilia cards were not just the most desirable cards – they were the *only* cards that had any profit for resellers. Buyers ignored any set that did not feature these premium cards. The manufacturers saw what the fans craved and squeezed every last dollar out of the concept. Soon there were cards with multiple autographs or bits of memorabilia. The most elaborate squeezed four players, each with their own signature and piece of jersey fabric, onto a single card.

As the market became centered around premium cards, super expensive sets that promised a signature or memorabilia card in every pack became increasingly popular. These decadent boxes, sometimes containing as few as four packs, could retail for $500. Remember, this is a product that once sold in candy stores for a nickel a pack!

Without a doubt, public interest could not keep up with the endless stream of products, and the industry crumbled accordingly. Once people felt safe buying on the internet, sports cards did rebound, especially single cards, as the shipping cost for these light items was not very high.

In the mid-90s, there were over 5000 stores that sold nothing but sports cards and memorabilia. Almost none exist today. The same is true of the companies that produced cards – where dozens once thrived, only a handful remain. In both cases, bankruptcy was common.

While autograph and memorabilia cards remain the most popular with true collectors, somewhere along the way kids regained interest in collecting the basic cards. This is evident from the shelves of large department stores. While the selection is limited, stores like Walmart always carry a selection of packs and boxes of sports cards at lower price points.

Sports cards are also still going strong online. On any given day, you can find thousands of listings on eBay, and it's all there, by the pack, box, or case. There are still plenty of collectors buying single cards as well, and you can find them at prices ranging from a penny to $50,000. But the days of dedicated sports card shops are essentially over. Collecting sports cards has again become a hobby for young boys and old men, conducted in private, far from the spotlight it once enjoyed.

Back before the internet transformed everything, there was a customer searching for a 1993 Topps Finest Mike Piazza rookie card. Rick came from a family of hardcore baseball fans. He wanted the card for his cousin, who had recently moved to California and become a Dodgers devotee. Rick was willing to pay $80 to get the Piazza rookie. I searched for it at many shows and eventually got one for $50. After I sold it to Rick for $70, he then had to mail it to California. His cousin received the card roughly a month after Rick asked me to find him one.

If Rick wanted that card today, he could spend fifteen minutes online and have it in his cousin's hands by the next day. There is no need to go on a quest through every nearby store and card show – which means there is no longer any need for dedicated card stores and shows.

At the height of the sports card boom there were too many different sets coming out to keep track of them all. For example, in a given season of baseball, one company called Topps would release *Opening Day*, *Stadium Club*, *Chrome*, *Topps Finest* and *Museum*, not to mention the regular Topps series 1 and 2 and the update series! The quality and price varied, as did the price of the randomly inserted chase cards. And that was just one of companies that manufactured baseball cards.

Dealers were always looking for the next big moneymaker and would risk everything to have the most. One such dealer was known as Mad Mike, who thought he had an infallible plan and let me in on it: He took out a $30,000 loan against his house so he could buy up all the *Pro Set Platinum*, an upcoming set of premium football cards.

Pro Set Platinum was just an upscale version of the regular Pro Set cards, which were low quality cards sold cheaply at K-Mart, Walmart, and even Blockbuster Video. Higher priced sets with super-premium cards were all the rage at the time, and when *Pro Set Platinum* came out boxes were selling for $55-60.

As Mike started to buy dealers out of their stock of *Pro Set Platinum*, the price kept climbing. Over the course of a major three day show, he bought every box he could. By the end he was paying as much as $80 and $90 a box. He figured that at next week's show he could easily get $100, maybe even $150 apiece.

When he arrived at the show next week, dealers were selling boxes of *Pro Set Platinum* for $40 each. Mad Mike wanted to buy them all since he could not sell the massive load he brought with him to the show. The problem was, he was broke from buying everybody out last week and was trying to borrow money or get the boxes of credit. Nobody was willing to take his offers, however, and he decided he would just have to bide his time until *Pro Set Platinum* boxes went back up in value.

One month later, at the same show they had been going for $40 each at, the price had dropped as low as $10. The dealer cost was $28, but since the set was so massed produced and available everywhere, dealers were taking what they could get. Not Mad Mike. He still had every box of *Pro Set Platinum* when they dipped under $10. Not long after that, Mad Mike had to close his store and get a job at Walmart.

The sport card industry still survives today, but it is not the sellers' market that it used to be. But I am happy that there are still fanatics out there eagerly trying to complete their collections. I am even happier that there are kids entering the hobby, free of the greed and corruption that permeated every form of collecting in the 90s. As for me, I still buy some new baseball, basketball, and football cards every season, just for the sheer, childlike joy of ripping open a pack of cards.

While sports cards have yet to recapture the popularity they once had, the same is not true for all trading cards. Trading card games, like every other former fad of the 90s, slowed down after the turn of the century. The majority of the games disappeared entirely, but the biggest are still around. *Magic: the Gathering*, the granddaddy of them all, has not only survived but surpassed its initial popularity.

Wizards of the Coast continue to release new *Magic* sets every year, maintaining a dedicated core of collectors and players that keep them afloat through thick and thin. *Pokémon*, on the other hand, went through a very rough time. During my store's final months, kids were coming in every day to try to sell their binders of cards for whatever they could get. But the *Pokémon* cartoons and video games have remained popular, so there was always a fan base, even though the cards had left a bad taste in many people's mouths that took years to wash out. Astonishingly enough, some of those binders full of *Pokémon* cards are worth more today than any point in the 90s!

Yu-Gi-Oh boosted the industry, bringing attention back to collectible card games in the new millennium. In addition, many kids who played *Yu-Gi-Oh* when it first came out eventually graduated to *Magic: The Gathering*. *Yu-Gi-Oh* retains a strong following today, and, like *Pokémon* and *Magic*, new sets are released regularly. *Magic* is more popular than ever, with tournaments that draw thousands and distribution numbers at an all-time high. You can still find regular *Yu-Gi-Oh* and *Pokémon* tournaments as well.

When I faced an endless stream of kids in my store, all trying to unload their *Pokémon* binders at any price they could get, it seemed like no one would ever again want to "catch them all". *Pokémon* cards were virtually worthless for several years, but eventually began to regain value – and they keep climbing! Boxes of the early sets fetch thousands, and a sealed box of first-edition base set cards recently sold for over $60,000, roughly two decades after it came out.

As we know, *Pokémon* as a franchise has evolved well beyond the card game, returning in new iterations like the *Pokémon Go* app. *Pokémon* storylines always revolved around exploration, but now Nintendo encourages kids to explore the real world around them, gaining navigational skills and exercise in the bargain. I think it is great that franchises can take on fresh life and engage new generations of fans who don't remember the dark side of these lighthearted games. For my part, I still play *Magic*, even occasionally attending a tournament, and I am happy to say that the game is as fun and challenging as ever.

While *Magic* and *Pokémon* have rebounded to new heights of popularity, this is not true of other iconic products. Beanie Babies, undoubtedly the biggest fad of the 90s, have had mixed success since then. Ty still sells Beanie Babies, though certainly not in the mind-boggling numbers that they did at their peak. Beanies have reverted to the product they were always supposed to be, cute little toys that appeal to kids and are easy to afford at a $6 to $8 price point.

Though Ty introduced several complementary product lines, trying to recapture the success of Beanie Babies, none of them ever did. The Beanies that sold for thousands of dollars in the 90s plummeted in value, understandably. For several years no one wanted anything to do with Beanies. That time of mourning has passed, however, and Beanies have made a bit of a comeback.

In recent years Ty has added licensed characters to the Beanie Babies lineup, including Marvel superheroes and cartoon characters like Garfield and Spongebob Squarepants. These sell well at retail but have not revived any interest in the secondary markets.

There may be some life in the original Beanies yet, however. A few of the oldest and rarest Beanie Babies are again creeping up in value – nowhere near where they were in the late 90s, or where they were predicted to be today, but there is still some hope. If people are shelling out top dollar for first-edition Charizards today, why not Valentinos or Erins or Princesses tomorrow? Regardless, with new Beanies still being released regularly, Beanie Babies have solidified a place in our culture, for better or worse.

Most of the smaller fads of the 90s haven't been so lucky. Furbys, for example, had a couple of brief reintroductions, but to no avail. Yomega yo-yos are a niche product again, unknown to all but the most devoted fans. Other properties, like Power Rangers, remain popular with kids but no longer attract collectors. And some things, like pogs, have vanished completely, little more than a footnote in the history of the 90s.

Of all the collectibles that appeared to be dying at end of the 90s, however, none has rebounded better than comic books. While sales of the physical books have never again approached the insane levels of "The Death of Superman" or early Image issues, this form of storytelling again has a solid footing in the culture. It's easier than ever for new generations of readers to get hooked, as libraries carry graphic novels and digital versions make both classic and current issues available at reasonable prices.

And of course, superheroes have exploded in mainstream popularity, as a series of incredibly successful movies and television shows have raked in profits. Second- and third-string properties like Iron Man, Wonder Woman, and Thor have now reached the iconic status of a Superman or Spider-Man, widely recognized by people who have never seen a minute of the movies or read a page of the comics.

This level of success was unimaginable at the turn of the century. In the late 90s, comic book companies were desperate to milk every possible dollar from what looked like the last gasps of their dying properties. They did things they would never have previously considered, such as a huge wave of inter-company crossovers. Batman teamed up with Spider-man, Superman fought the Hulk, and eventually the Justice League of America and the Avengers faced off in a final cash grab. These efforts were not too warmly received, but were far from the only ways that comic companies tried to wring profit from their holdings.

Marvel, needing cash to claw their way out of bankruptcy, sold off the movie rights to all their characters. Superhero movies have always existed, though costumes and abilities that looked awesome in the books often appeared corny and embarrassing on the screen. Lo and behold, with the new millennium came improvements in technology that made competent superhero movies feasible.

Beginning with *Blade*, a little-known vampire hero, Marvel enjoyed a string of successful films featuring their characters. *X-Men* followed *Blade*, which led to the first *Spider-Man* movie. These movies were all great successes, earning Marvel huge box office scores and bringing new interest to their characters.

Two decades later, comic book movies dominate Hollywood. DC got into the game with a trio of critically and commercially successful Batman movies. Marvel went a step further, regaining control of most of their properties and joining them into one unified film series. As I write this, the Marvel Cinematic Universe has become the most commercially successful film franchise of all time, with profits in the billions.

While comic books themselves almost feel outdated at this point, the comics industry has changed, and so has collecting. Old Superman and Batman comics have never stopped being desirable and are worth more than ever now. But their exact worth has always been based on a subjective judgment of condition that sometimes varied widely between buyers and sellers.

No longer, because professional grading has arrived. The process is simple enough: you send off your best comics to one of several qualified companies, who assign a numerical grade to the condition of the book, then lock it away in an airtight plastic slab. This helps protect the book, of course, but also gives collectors a baseline for trading and selling. There is no debate about the book's condition, and no chance that it will change.

For older comics, graded issues have become the preferred way to buy and sell, and having a certified top grade on a key older book ensures you will make much more than you could have ever gotten before. Grading is important for the preservation of old comics, but it is not just the books of the 60s and 70s that are being graded in order to fetch profits. Some of the most overprinted 90s issues can be worth a pretty penny in perfect grade. And then there are the fans who send out new comics, rushing them off to get graded the day they come out!

New comics today are not all that different than they used to be, though there have been some notable updates. The major companies have all tried to keep up with technology by offering downloadable digital versions. Digital comics haven't exactly revolutionized the industry but are a popular way to enjoy the books, especially if you just want to read the stories without lugging around boxes full of bagged and boarded issues.

Marvel and DC have also launched a number of reboots to their comic universes in an attempt to make them more accessible to new fans. New and different heroes stand alongside the classics, and some of the most iconic characters have different faces behind the mask than you might remember. While sales are still much lower than in the boom years, the comic book industry is quite healthy these days.

Since I first discovered them in my grandfather's store, I have never stopped reading comic books. I think there are still many great titles coming out today. Most publishers have tried to introduce more diversity into their comics, both in terms of characters and creators. This is a welcome change. These companies have adapted to the needs of a new millennium, rescuing the industry from the brink of obscurity.

The industry is even strong enough to support some comebacks beyond the Big Two, including the surprising resurrection of Valiant Comics. After years in limbo, the company made a powerful return in 2012, reviving all their classic characters. Now, Valiant publishes more titles than at any point in their history, proving that nothing really dies, only changes.

Except Pogs, which are still quite dead.

One aspect of the 90s that I absolutely do not miss is what I call "the phenomenon of disuse". Traditionally, people became collectors because they simply fell in love with some type of item, but in the 90s these fans were few and far between. During that decade, most of the people jumping into collecting only cared about one thing: money. And since condition is everything to collectors, this meant that a large percentage of the products went directly into storage, never to be used.

As an example, let's take a look at three of my sports card regulars. Big Ed, a lifelong collector and Yankees fan, was ecstatic if he pulled a Yankee player's card from a pack. Barry, the gambler, would hastily dig through a pack for pricey cards and abandon the rest on my table. And Andy, the "smart" investor, stashed the unopened pack in his closet to await a rise in value.

Of these three collectors, only Big Ed got any joy from his cards beyond a theoretical selling price. Most of my customers resembled Barry and Andy, mechanically storing away their unloved cards, if not throwing them out entirely.

The phenomenon was not limited to trading cards. People were stashing away anything they could get their hands on, thinking that it would make them millions within a few years. Even though I enjoyed selling the stuff, it really saddened me knowing that most of it was going to be put into a closet or storage space without a second thought.

One thing that I loved about selling comic books was that I got to read everything as it came out. Comics were always meant to be read, after which they could be stored away to keep them in great shape for years to come. But during the boom, most did not even give their issues that first read. I had a regular comic buyer who picked up all the hot issues from me. One day I asked him what he thought of *Spawn* #1. To my surprise, he replied that he never once read a comic he bought from me. He simply put them away, thinking it was better than money in the bank.

At least most of the people buying *Magic: The Gathering* cards actually played the game. But even *Magic* attracted its fair share of speculators, especially in the earlier days. There were plenty of sports card collectors who would try to complete full sets of *Magic* and stash them away. Come to think of it, if those people still have those sets, they actually stand to make some money from them.

When it came to *Pokémon*, however, the phenomenon of disuse was much more prevalent. It broke my heart sometimes, but most of the *Pokémon* cards I sold ended up in the hands of kids who had no desire to play the game. Some just enjoyed collecting and looking at the cards, which is fine, but plenty had bigger dreams. Time and time again I saw kids making their purchases with that glint in their eye that told me they thought the cards were going to make them rich. Usually they held onto a card for a couple of weeks until they saw I didn't have one in the case, at which point they'd try to re-sell it for a higher price. I could never pay more than what I sold it for, so time and time again they went home defeated, cards in hand and tears in eye.

Beanie Babies had the same problem. They were a child's toy in design but became more valuable than gold. This led to many kids wanting to cash in on the fad too, refraining from enjoying their stuffed animals in hopes of making profits down the line. The parents were really to blame, however. I heard so many parents tell their kids that the Beanies they were buying for them were not to be played with. I even gave my own son the same advice, though he was wise enough to completely ignore me. Unlike most kids, he ripped off those tags and enjoyed playing with his Beanie Babies to the fullest extent, unconcerned with monetary worth, as any kid should be.

Perhaps the saddest moment was when I had a lady come in to my store regularly with her daughters. She let them each pick a Beanie Baby from the $5 table. Even with Beanies at their height, you might think that for $5 she would let the kids play with them. But no, this was not the case. She told me many times that she kept the Beanies in giant tubs, each in its own plastic zip bag. She thought she was doing the right thing by not letting her daughters play with them or even touch them. She said that they were going to pay for her daughters' college education someday.

Part of the problem was that throughout the 1980s and 1990s, everyone saw news stories about skyrocketing values for pristine toys and comics from earlier eras. But because collecting things like toys and comics was not widespread in those decades, most of the items sold in those years had been read or played with, used up, and tossed out. The high prices came because the items were truly rare.

But then the public caught on, and everybody was stashing sealed product in their closets. There was nothing rare about having a perfect copy of a comic when everyone else had a dozen of their own, and no one wanted to read them.

In the year 2000, I had some random dude come into my store with a collection of Batman action figures, all mint in the original packaging. He had been collecting them for the last decade, starting with the 1989 movie right up to the most recent releases. Buying them at retail, he had paid $5 to $10 each – and that was still what they were worth.

I didn't want to insult him, but my best offer was $3 a figure. I guess it was the best offer he got anywhere, because two months later he came back asking if I'd still do the deal. He had even more figures by then, and I gave him $750 for the lot of them. I sold them for $5 each at flea markets and sold out within a few months. The best thing about that deal was that almost all the figures went to young children, who ripped them right out of the package. Toys should be played with, not left to collect dust in some old guy's closet.

There are still plenty of adult collectors out there stashing everything away, unopened, the moment they get it. But I think the phenomenon of disuse is past its peak, fortunately. People realized that you can't just store away any random toy store purchase and make money from it in a couple of years. Toys are, for the most part, just for kids now. Comic books are being read again, stuffed animals are in more beds than storage facilities, and trading card games are actually being played.

All things considered, the 90s fallout could have been much worse. It is great that many of the products survived. Too bad the same can't be said for all the small businesses that sold those products. The further we get from the 90s, the further we also get from buying stuff in actual, tangible stores and markets. Spending a day walking around a hot flea market or crowded collectible show while searching for that one special item has become a quaint memory for us older folks, and it's an experience the newer generations will never have.

Why even leave the house when you can find a much wider selection and better prices from your couch? Although many 90s products are still around, the 90s lifestyle is fading further into the past, one screen tap at a time. But the memories are all a click away, affordably priced, with an option for next-day shipping.

43987106R00106

Made in the USA
Middletown, DE
04 May 2019